联合早报

熟语大家学

Learn Chinese The Fun Way

汪惠迪　辑

谢世顺　译

梁锦泉
黄志强　插图
林德生

联邦出版社・联合早报

A member of the Times Publishing Group
Times Centre
1 New Industrial Road
Singapore 1953

1993年初版
1994年6月再版

ISBN 981 01 3039 2

Printed in Singapore by Chong Moh Offset Printing Pte Ltd

目 录

成语

俗语

惯用语

歇后语

败走麦城 bài zǒu Màichéng

麦城：中国古代地名，在现今湖北省当阳县东南的沮（jǔ）水和漳水之间。东汉建安24年（公元219年），蜀汉大将关羽被东吴的吕蒙打败，退守麦城，在突围时被俘，最后给孙权杀掉。“败走麦城”比喻受挫折或遭惨败。例如：中国女选手黄华、唐九红均在半决赛中负于印尼选手，使中国自1982年以来首次无人进入女单决赛。在女双比赛中，中国队败走“麦城”，两队双打在复赛中失利。（《印尼威胁中国霸业——全英羽球公开赛评述》，1991年3月19日《联合早报》第22版）

To Be Thoroughly Defeated At Maicheng

China's celebrated general Guan Yu was defeated by his enemy and killed at Maicheng, a city in Central China in 219 AD. This Chinese idiom originated from that historical event. It is similar in meaning to the English idiom: "Meet one's Waterloo".

Example: "In the recent badminton match with Indonesia, China's woman players failed for the first time since 1982 to enter the single finals. In the woman's doubles, they too have been 'thoroughly defeated at Maicheng'." (Lianhe Zaobao 19/3/91)

兵连祸结 bīng lián huò jié

兵：指战争；连：连续、接连；祸：灾祸；结：联在一起。

这条成语的意思是，战争接连不断，灾祸连着出现。例如：兵连祸结经济受损/波斯湾国家叫苦连天（标题，1991年2月4日《联合早报》第17版）

这条成语也说成“祸结兵连”或“兵连祸深”。

Ravaged By Successive Wars

“Bing” refers figuratively to war, while “huo” means disaster. This Chinese idiom describes how wars erupt one after another, resulting in disaster and hardship for the people.

Example: A headline in Lianhe Zaobao on 4/2/91 described the situation in the Middle East as ‘Ravaged by successive wars’, Gulf countries are pouring out endless grievances.

抽刀断水 chōu dāo duàn shuǐ

抽出刀来要斩断流水，比喻对事情毫无帮助，解决不了问题，甚至会加速事态的发展。这条成语出自唐朝诗人李白的诗句："抽刀断水水更流，举杯消愁愁更愁"。

在过去60年中，泰国发生了20次政变，平均三年一场。1991年4月21日《联合早报》星期刊的专题报道，题目便是"抽刀断水"。作者用这条成语来形容泰国的政变，意思是政变在泰国没完没了。（详见该日早报第17版）

To Chop The Water To Stop Its Flow

The Chinese idiom describes a futile effort to check the deterioration of an adverse trend or situation which apparently only makes it worse.

This idiom was used as a headline for a special feature article in Sunday Zaobao (21/4/91) to describe actions taken by Thailand to check more military coups, which occurred once every three years since the 1930s.

得意门生 déyì ménshēng

得意：称心如意；门生：学生。指最满意、最受欣赏的学生或徒弟。例如：库恩斯（德裔〔yì〕美国雕塑家）说，为了和小白菜（意大利肉弹议员）结婚，他不仅收到一些恐吓（kǒnghè）信，连他的一些得意门生也离开了他。（《小白菜嫁“洋”乃武》，1991年6月3日《联合早报》第26版）。

Most Outstanding Students

This Chinese idiom is commonly used by teachers to describe students or disciples whom they like best because they show outstanding qualities.

Example: “American sculptor, Jeff Koons said that after he decided to marry Italian porn star Stallar, he received several letters of threat, and even some of his ‘most outstanding students’ have left him.” (Lianhe Zaobao 3/6/91)

分庭抗礼 fēn tíng kàng lǐ

庭：庭院；抗：对等、相当。古代宾客和主人分别站在庭院中的两边，相对行礼，以平等的地位相待，比喻彼此以平等或对等的关系相处，不分高低或上下。

现在用这条成语常指互相对立。例如：总理公署高级部长李光耀前往东京参加明仁天皇登基典礼期间，曾接受日本《朝日月刊》的访问。他指出，对金日成、越南人和中国来说，国际局势已经改变，再也没有一个东方集团同美国及西欧分庭抗礼了。（《接受日本《朝日月刊》访问/李光耀谈世界秩序》，1990年12月7日《联合早报》第11版）

“分庭抗礼”也还可以指搞分裂、闹独立的言行。

To Make Rival Claims As An Equal

"Ting" refers to the reception hall of a building. In ancient etiquette, the host and guest would stand on each side of the hall to greet each other as equals. Nowadays, this Chinese idiom is generally used to refer to two rivals standing up against each other as equals.

Example: "Senior Minister Lee Kuan Yew told 'Asahi Monthly' that the international situation has greatly altered and as far as Kim II Sung, or the Vietnamese and Chinese are concerned, there is no longer any Eastern Bloc 'to make rival claims as an equal' to the US and Western Europe." (Lianhe Zaobao 7/12/90)

分一杯羹　fēn yī bēi gēng

羹：汤类食物，这里指肉汁。

秦朝末年，楚（项羽）汉（刘邦）相争，刘邦的父亲被项羽俘虏。后来双方的军队相持不下，项羽就派人对刘邦说，要是还不赶快投降，就要把他的父亲当作肉一样来烹煮了。刘邦回答说，一定要烹煮的话，到时候希望分给我一杯肉汁。因此，这条成语的意思是"分享利益"。例如：战后科威特重建以及各国补充更新军事装备甚至重建伊拉克时，英国有理由期望分到一杯羹。（《英国参战何所得》，1991年3月6日《联合早报》第13版）

这一条成语也说成"分我杯羹"或紧缩说成"分羹"。

To Share The Spoils

This Chinese idiom originated from an ancient story in China in which Xiang Yu, a courageous general threatened to boil his rival, Liu Bang's father alive. Liu, who later became the first emperor of the Han dynasty, replied defiantly, "If you insist on boiling him, please do let me have a share of the broth." The idiom is now used to mean sharing the spoils.

Example: "The reconstruction of Kuwait and supply of fresh defence equipment to the Gulf states offer foreign countries many business opportunities; for Britain, it has good reason to demand 'a share of the spoils'." (Lianhe Zaobao 6/3/91)

风马牛不相及 fēng mǎ niú bù xiāng jí

风：牲畜发情，公母互相追逐。及：碰头。马和牛不同类，不会互相引诱、追逐。因此，这条成语是比喻两种事物丝毫不相干。例如：法国南部蒙彼利埃有一家名叫巴格达的咖啡店。美伊战争爆发后，不但顾客大减，店主还不断接到恐吓电话，于是不得不改换招牌。其实这家咖啡店跟伊拉克风马牛不相及。（《炸弹“爱”巴格达·店主被迫改名》，1991年1月29日《新明日报》第7版）

这条成语也说成“风马牛不相接”，或“风马不接”（接：接触”）。还可以进一步减省，说成“风马牛”、“马牛风”或“牛马风”，甚至只要两个字，说成“风马”。

Have Absolutely Nothing To Do With Each Other

“Feng” here refers to the sexual craving of animals. This Chinese proverb uses the difference in nature between the mare and the cow to emphasise the irrelevancy of two things.

Example: “A coffee house in Montbeliard, France was known as Baghdad. Since the Gulf War, its owner had been receiving threatening calls and was forced to change the name. Actually, the coffee house and Iraq ‘have absolutely nothing to do with each other’.” (Shin Min Daily News 29/1/91)

更上一层楼 gèng shàng yī céng lóu

"欲穷千里目，更上一层楼"这是中国唐朝诗人王之涣 (huàn) 写的五言绝句里的后两句，意思是想看得更远，就要登得更高。（"五言绝句"是中国的一种旧体诗，一首四句，每句五个字。）

这条成语比喻再提高或前进一步。例如：新加坡从建国以来，治国者的精明能干是国家进步繁荣的主要推动力，未来能否更上一层楼，就看民间能否发挥更大的积极性和爱国心。（《"公民社会"的真谛》，1991年6月23日《联合早报》第2版）

在鼓励人家时，常用这条成语。

To Move To A Higher Plane

This Chinese term originated from a poem which literally means that one has to climb up to a higher storey in order to enjoy a panoramic view of the beautiful scenery. It's now commonly used to describe an extra effort to attain greater achievement.

Example: "Singapore's progress and prosperity since independence is due mainly to the acumen and capability of its administrators who are a motivating force. However, for the country 'to move to a higher plane', the people must now bring into play their positive attitudes and patriotism." (Lianhe Zaobao 23/6/91)

孤注一掷 gū zhù yī zhì

孤注：注是赌博时所下的钱；孤注是赌钱的人在钱快输完时把所有的钱当作一注押上去。一掷：指赌钱时掷色子（shǎizi）；一掷是最后一次掷色子，以决输赢。

这个成语是比喻使出全部力量，作最后的一次冒险。例如：沙巴州执政的团结党突然退出国阵，而加入反对党46精神党的阵营……对沙巴团结党领袖，也是首席部长的百林来说，这无疑是"孤注一掷"的做法，沙巴州在大选后是否能够争取到他们向来所要争取的权益，还得看大马政权落入谁的手里。（《沙巴团结党"孤注一掷"》，1990年10月18日《联合早报》社论）

Place Everything On One Single Stake

This Chinese idiom means to stake one's entire fortune on a single chance or to bet all on a single throw. It is used usually to describe how a person is embarking on a win-all or lose-all venture.

Example: "The decision by Sabah's ruling party, PBS to withdraw from the National Front and join the opposition shows that Chief Minister Pairin is 'placing everything on one single stake': whether he can win more rights for the state depends wholly on the election results." (Lianhe Zaobao 18/10/90)

古道热肠 gǔ dào rè cháng

也说“热肠古道”。古道：古代淳朴厚道的风俗习惯；热肠：热心肠。这个成语形容待人真挚、热情，并且乐于帮助他人。例如：儿获奖学金・父捐款做慈善/冰水小贩李鹤枝古道热肠。（标题，1990年10月11日《联合早报》第4版）

Old Virtues And Warm Bowels

This is the literal translation of the Chinese idiom which emphasises a person's warm bloodedness and strong belief in old virtues: truthful, sympathetic and a readiness to help others.

Example: “Soft drink hawker Li Hezhi whose son has just received a scholarship, donated the money to charity, he is indeed a man of ‘old virtues and warm bowels’.” (Lianhe Wanbao 11/10/90)

继往开来 jì wǎng kāi lái

这条成语也许是“继往圣，开来学”的简缩。“继往圣，开来学”是指继承以往圣贤的学说，并为未来的学业开拓（kāituò，开辟〔pì〕、扩展）道路。

继往开来的意思是，继承前人的事业，开辟未来的道路。例如：公民咨询委员会七大分区主席，在晚宴上赠送一幅刻有“继往开来”的匾额（biǎn'é）予吴总理，这是出自书法家潘受的墨宝。（《吴总理宣布教育储蓄计划/人人同时起步机会均等》，1990年12月18日《联合早报》封面版）

“继”也说“嗣”（sì，继承）或“绍”（继续、继承）；“继往开来”也可以简缩说成“开继”。

Carry Forward The Cause And Forge Ahead Into The Future

This Chinese idiom originally meant to inherit the teachings of past saints so as to help students develop their future. It is generally used nowadays to describe someone who takes over the task from his predecessor and continues to strive for greater achievement.

Example: “The chairmen of seven major Citizen Consultative Committees presented a plaque to PM Goh at the dinner. The message on the plaque was written by calligrapher Pan Shou, which means, ‘carry forward the cause and forge ahead into the future’.” (Lianhe Zaobao 18/12/90)

见贤思齐 jiàn xián sī qí

贤：有道德、有才能的人。齐：相等、相同。看到有道德、有才能的人，就向他学习，想办法赶上他。例如：一个国家要进步，就得往外看，“见贤思齐”，往外取经。把某个国家当作特定学习运动的对象，也是一种潮流。（《见贤思齐，往外取经》，1991年5月26日《联合早报》第2版）

也说成“见德思齐”或“怀贤思齐”（怀：心里存有）。

To Learn From People Who Are More Superior

"Xian" refers to people who are capable and morally upright. This Chinese idiom means when we meet people who are more superior than us in character, we should emulate them.

Example: "When a country is striving for progress, it should be outward-looking and 'to learn from people who are more superior'. It is now quite a common practice to hold up a certain country as a good example for emulation." (Lianhe Zaobao 26/5/91)

急功近利 jí gōng jìn lì

功：成绩、成效；近：眼前的；利：利益。指急着争取眼前的成效和利益。例如：李资政说，我国的工人，特别是年轻工人的缺点是急功近利，缺乏耐心。我们必须改变这种态度，才能成为训练有素的工人。（《工会今后应注重工人教育与训练》，1991年5月5日《联合早报》第6版）

这条成语也说成“急效近功”、“近效急功”、“急功近名”或“浅功近利”。

Eager For Quick Success And Instant Benefit

This Chinese idiom is commonly used to describe people who are impatient to win recognition and achieve tangible results within the shortest possible time.

Example: “Senior Minister Lee Kuan Yew said Singapore’s workers, particularly those who are young, are ‘eager for quick success and instant benefit’. He advised them to change their attitude so as to become well-trained workers.” (Lianhe Zaobao 5/5/91)

镜花水月 jìng huā shuǐ yuè

镜子里的花，水里的月亮。比喻虚幻的东西（虚幻：xūhuàn，不真实的）。例如：新机场原本是香港内部建设项目，如今演变成中英外交层次共管的事务。因此，有人认为，这个模式将使香港1997年后的高度自治、港人治港成为镜花水月。（《对中英新机场协议，香港各界褒贬之一》，1991年7月6日《联合早报》第2版。褒贬：bāobiǎn，评论好坏。）

这条俗语也说成"镜像水月"（或"水月镜像"）或"水月镜花"。

Flowers In A Mirror Or The Moon In The Water

This Chinese idiom is commonly used to describe something that is nothing more than an illusion.

Example: "Hong Kong's proposed new airport project was originally a domestic affair, but it has now become a diplomatic tussle between China and Britain. Some people are worried that under these circumstances, the prospect of a highly-autonomous HK ruled by Hongkongers is like 'flowers in a mirror or the moon in the water'." (Lianhe Zaobao 6/7/91)

具体而微 jù tǐ ér wēi

具体：大体具备；微：微小。这条成语的意思是内容大体具备，不过规模、布局比较小或显得不怎么突出。例如：《联合早报》发表了一篇介绍本地一家模型制作公司的特写，题目是“模型艺术具体而微”（1991年3月4日第4版）。

Small Yet Complete

“Ju ti” means complete or comprehensive: “Wei” is small or tiny. This Chinese idiom is used to describe something which is small in size but is complete and comprehensive in substance.

Example: In an article on 4/3/91 introducing a company specialising in miniature building models. Lianhe Zaobao headlined: “The art of making models, ‘small yet complete’.”

开门揖盗　kāi mén yī dào

揖：作揖，两手抱拳高举，身子略弯，向人敬礼；表示欢迎。这条成语的意思是打开大门迎接强盗，比喻引进坏人，自己招来祸患。例如：有一个强盗假装送货员上门送礼物，一名家庭主妇信以为真，开门将强盗迎进屋里。这时，强盗露出本相，用刀威胁（wēixié）她，抢走1000多元财物。《新明日报》在报道这一则新闻时，标题是"劫匪假冒送货员·主妇失察开门揖盗"。（1990年12月8日第5版，失察：疏忽、不小心）

"揖"也说"延"（引进、迎接）。"揖盗"也说"纳寇"（nàkòu 纳：放进来；寇：强盗或侵略者）或"纳狼"（狼比喻坏人）。

"开门揖盗"还可以省去"开门"，单说"揖盗"。

Open The Door To Greet The Robber

"Yi" is the traditional Chinese way of bowing as a gesture of welcome. This Chinese idiom satirizes someone who invites disaster by letting in evildoers.

It was used as a headline to describe how a robber under the pretext of delivering some gifts, tricked a housewife into opening the door and robbed her of $1000 worth of cash and valuables. She was said to have 'opened the door to greet the robber'. (Shin Min Daily News 8/12/90)

看风使舵 kàn fēng shǐ duò

使：使用。这条成语比喻做事随着情况的变化而灵活地应付（通常含贬意）。例如：陈太太说，有些巴杀的小贩，很会看风使舵。他们知道顾客是香港人，就故意算贵一点。（《“41号大酒店”里的小故事》，1991年6月8日《联合早报》第7版）

“看风”也说“见风”、“随风”、“相（xiàng，仔细看）风”或“占（zhān，预测）风”；“使舵”也说“使帆”、“转舵”、“倒舵”、“行（xíng）船”、“使船”或“驶船”。

To Trim One's Sails

Figuratively, this Chinese idiom means to act according to different or changing circumstances.

Example: "Mrs Cheng said that some hawkers in the market certainly knew how 'to trim their sails': when they realised that the customers were from Hongkong, they immediately jacked up the prices." (Lianhe Zaobao 8/6/91)

立竿见影　lì gān jiàn yǐng

把竹竿竖在太阳光下，立刻就看到它的影子。比喻收效迅速。例如：这些措施对农业产生了立竿见影的效果，不但作物产量接连几年都持续增加，副产品的生产也普遍提升。（《中国的粮产问题 / 增长的趋向及其意义》，1991年7月6日《联合早报》第14版）

To Produce Instant Results

Literally, this Chinese idiom means to set up a pole under the sun and see its shadow.

Example: "These measures 'produced instant results' for the agricultural industry. Not only has farm production increased continuously in the last few years, even the quantity of by-products has been boosted greatly." (Lianhe Zaobao 6/7/91)

瞒天过海 mán tiān guò hǎi

指用欺骗的手法暗中活动。例如：三个尼日利亚人把4.14公斤海洛英分藏在12个密封的爽身粉罐子里，然后放进行李袋，跟25罐真爽身粉混在一起，想瞒天过海，把这批毒品转运到欧洲去，前天下午在樟宜机场被中央肃毒局人员逮捕。（《爽身粉罐内藏毒品，三尼日利亚人被捕》，1991年6月8日《联合早报》第2版）

To Practise Deception Boldly

Literally, this Chinese idiom means to cross the sea by a trick. It is generally used to describe people who carry out illegal activities secretly.

Example: "Three Nigerians attempted to smuggle 4.14 kg of heroine to Europe by concealing them in 12 tightly-sealed talcum powder containers, and placed them together with another 25 containers of genuine talcum powder. They were really trying 'to practise deception boldly', but were finally arrested at Changi Airport." (Lianhe Zaobao 8/6/91)

冒天下之大不韪 mào tiānxià zhī dà bùwěi

冒：犯；之：的；不韪：错误。意思是犯了天下最大的错误。现在引用这条成语大多指不顾世人的反对而干坏事。例如：伊拉克敢冒天下之大不韪，一夜之间吞并了科威特。（《美国什锦》，1990年11月23日《联合早报》第21版）

这条成语也说成“犯天下之不韪”。

To Risk Universal Condemnation

"Mao" means to go against; "da buwei" is grave error or serious crime. Literally, this Chinese saying means to commit the greatest error on earth. It is commonly used to describe someone who defies world opinion and openly commits a crime.

Example: "Iraq 'risked universal condemnation' by annexing Kuwait overnight." (Lianhe Zaobao 23/11/90)

蜻蜓点水 qīngtíng diǎn shuǐ

点水：以极快的速度略微触一下水面。蜻蜓的幼体须生活在水中，蜻蜓在产卵时就将尾巴轻触水面。这条成语是比喻做事情只是浮面接触，不深入。例如：在美国，凡是高级住宅区必有华人居所。有些地段，一个家族便拥有几栋房子，号称“某家村”，近乎招摇。至于“太空人”充斥，华屋美厦一年只蜻蜓点水似地住几天，此外长年空置，这种现象，也会招人非议。（《华人应该改变形象》，1991年3月21日《联合早报》第14版）

Like A Dragonfly Skimming The Surface Of The Water

Figuratively, this Chinese idiom describes an action which touches on the subject superficially without going into it in any depth.

Example: “Many overseas Chinese own luxurious houses in the United States. In some cases, one family may even own several houses. For those who have to travel frequently especially, they stay in the house only for a few days in one whole year, just ‘like a dragonfly skimming the surface of the water’. Such wasteful practice is bound to invite criticism.” (Lianhe Zaobao 21/3/91)

秋后算帐 qiū hòu suàn zhàng

秋后：秋季农作物收获以后；算帐：计算产量和产值。原指农业上每年的收成要到大秋（九、十月收割玉米、高粱等作物的季节）之后才算总帐。它有两个比喻义：一是等到事情有了结果时，才来判断是非、曲直或正误；一是在政治斗争中等待机会跟对方算总帐，即伺（sì）机报复。例如：1989年7月初，查良镛在接受美联社的一次访问时说："如果97年后我还留在香港，恐怕他们（中国共产党）会秋后算帐。这会很危险，我为自己和太太担心。"（《金庸封剑归隐？》，《联合早报》1991年3月20日第19版）。这个例句中的"秋后算帐"用的是第二个比喻意义。

To Square Accounts After The Autumn Harvest

In China, the main harvest takes place in autumn and all outstanding accounts are normally settled after that period. This idiom either means to set things straight after the event is over; or in politics, to deal harshly with the opponents after the political struggle is over.

Example: "Novelist Zha Liangyong told AP in an interview that if he stayed behind in HK after 1997, the Chinese Communist Party might want to 'square accounts after the autumn harvest,' he and his wife were therefore very worried." (Lianhe Zaobao 20/3/91)

群龙无首 qún lóng wú shǒu

一群龙没有一个带头的，比喻一群人当中没有一个领头的，即无人领导。例如：拉吉夫遇害后，有106年历史的国大党目前群龙无首，数十名国大党领袖可能再要求原籍意大利的拉吉夫遗孀苏妮娅出任党主席。（《国大党可能再要求苏妮娅出任党主席》，1991年5月26日《联合早报》第36版）

A Group Without A Leader

Literally, this Chinese idiom means a host of dragons without a head (leader).

Example: "After the assassination of Rajiv Gandhi, the 106-year old Congress Party became 'a group without a leader', and many party elders asked Mr Gandhi's widow, Sonia to reconsider the party's offer to be the new chairman." (Lianhe Zaobao 26/5/91)

任人唯才 rèn rén wéi cái

任：任用；唯：只；才：才能。这条成语的意思是，任用人只选择那些才能出众（chūzhòng，比众人高）的人，不管这个人跟自己的关系是不是密切。例如：我提出这个教育储蓄计划，目的是要给我们一向奉行的任人唯才的自由市场制度注入一些温情和提供更多的均等机会。在这个自由市场制度下，有才干的人会受到鼓励，尽量发挥所长。（吴作栋总理在公民咨询委员会宴会上的讲话，1990年12月18日《联合早报》第8版）

跟“任人唯才”意思相近的还有“任人唯贤”。“贤”指有才有德。“任人唯贤”是指任用人只以德才兼备为标准，不管这个人跟自己的关系是不是密切。

如果说成“任人唯亲”，是指任用人不管德与才怎样，只选择那些跟自己感情好、关系密切的人。

Appoint People On Their Merits

This Chinese idiom has become the common Chinese translation for “meritocracy” as practised in Singapore. It means to appoint people according to their personal integrity and abilities.

Example: “The reason Edusave is proposed is to introduce an element of compassion and more equal opportunities for everyone in our free market system in which we ‘appoint people according to their merits’. Under the system, all persons of calibre are encouraged to put their talents to maximum use.” (Lianhe Zaobao 18/12/90)

锐不可当 ruì bù kě dāng

锐：锋利；当：抵挡；锐也说锋，锋指兵器的尖端或军队的前列。

“锐不可当”或“锋不可当”都是形容气势威猛，不可阻挡。例如：李光耀总理指出，美国报章发觉到，尽管它们在国内有排山倒海的力量，但它们在新加坡这样的第三世界国家里，却并不是一股锐不可当的力量。（《美报章并非锐不可当》，1990年10月16日《联合早报》）

这个成语也说成“锋锐未可当”或“锐未可当”。

An Irresistible Force

The word “Rui” means sharpness or incisiveness. It is usually used to describe the sharp point of a weapon or the spearhead of an advancing army and penetrating force is so powerful that it seems to be irresistible and unstoppable.

Example: “Prime Minister Lee Kuan Yew said that while they (the US press) could move mountains in Washington, they were not ‘an irresistible force’ in a foreign Third World country like Singapore.” (Lianhe Zaobao 16/10/90)

煞有介事　shà yǒu jiè shì

常说成“像煞有介事”，上海方言词语，已被华语词汇吸收。

像煞：很像、像极了；介事：那样的事情。这条成语的意思是好像真有那回事似的。例如：美国大兵这次到沙漠，不好玩了，没有女人，没有电视，没有冰啤酒，怎么办？有的大兵用纸板作了假电视机、假电话、假冷风机，他们还煞有介事地在冷风机旁享受着嗖嗖（sōu，音搜）冷风。（《美国什锦》，1990年11月23日《联合早报》第21版）

Make It Feel Like The Real Thing

This Chinese idiom originated from the Shanghai dialect which describes an action that is put up ostentatiously to show as if it is done in earnest.

Example: “The American soldiers in the desert are feeling bored without women, TV and cool beer. To assuage their boredom, they made TV sets, telephones and air-conditioners out of cardboard, and even sit beside the air-conditioners to enjoy the cool air to ‘make it feel like the real thing’.” (Lianhe Zaobao 23/11/90)

水落石出 shuǐ luò shí chū

水落下去，石头就露出来，原本用来形容水枯季节的自然景色，现在都用来比喻事情真相大白。例如：印度政府前天说，拉吉夫遭暗杀是一个经过详細策划的阴谋，当局决心查个水落石出。（《印度政府：暗杀拉吉夫行动，事先经过详細策划》，1991年5月28日《联合早报》第32版）

也说成“水清石见（现）”、“水清石出”或“水涸（hé，水干了）石出”。

When The Water Subsides The Rocks Emerge

Originally, this Chinese idiom was a description of natural scenery, but it is now figuratively used to describe something that has finally come to light.

Example: “The Indian government said that the assassination of Rajiv Gandhi was a carefully plotted conspiracy and it was determined to investigate until ‘the water subsided and the rocks emerged’.” (Lianhe Zaobao 28/5/91)

水乳交融 shuǐ rǔ jiāo róng

乳：奶汁；交融：融合在一起。水和乳汁融合在一起，比喻关系非常密切或结合得十分紧密。例如：汉藏两族的关系早就水乳交融了，否则，藏族的先人（祖先）是不可能把汉族的公主抽象成为文学人物的，更何况是史诗人物呢。（《西藏独立和"与狼共舞"》，1991年5月27日《联合早报》第17版）

也说成"水乳相和（huò）"。

As Well Blended As Milk And Water

This Chinese idiom is commonly used to describe the relationship between two persons who are in complete harmony.

Example: "The relationship between the Hans and Tibetans in China has always been 'as well blended as milk and water', or else, the ancestors of the Tibetans would not have depicted Han princesses as characters in their literature and even in the epics." (Lianhe Zaobao 27/5/91)

说三道四　shuō sān dào sì

说这说那，胡乱议论。例如：一名正在瑞士日内瓦出席联合国会议的中国官员前日重申，北京对六四民运分子的审判，是中国内部事务，不容许外国政府、组织或个人“说三道四”。（《中国代表在联合国人权会上说/审民运分子属内政・不容许外国人干涉》，1991年2月22日《联合早报》第31版）

这条成语也说成“言三语四”。

To Comment Critically

This Chinese idiom means to comment on certain events with disapproval.

Example: “A Chinese official who was in Geneva attending a UN conference reiterated that the trial of pro-democracy movement leaders in Beijing was a domestic affair and China would not allow foreign governments, organisations or individuals ‘to comment critically’ on its action.” (Lianhe Zaobao 22/2/91)

天高皇帝远　tiān gāo huángdì yuǎn

比喻偏远的地区，中央政府的法令达不到，权力管不着；也说成“山高皇帝远”。例如：美国是移民者向往的国度，许多人以为公民的义务只是纳税。他们连选举权都放弃——天高皇帝远，谁当官跟我有什么关系？（《美国华裔效忠美国吗？》，1991年3月5日《联合早报》第12版）

Out Of Reach Of The Authorities

Literally, this Chinese idiom means the God is high above and the emperor is far away. It is used to describe places which are very remote and the laws of the central authorities cannot be effectively enforced.

Example: "The United States of America is a favourite country for many migrants as most of them think the only obligation as a US citizen is paying taxes. They are not interested in any rights, not even the right to vote. They seem to think that they are 'out of reach of the authorities' and as to who comes into power, what has it to do with them?" (Lianhe Zaobao 5/3/91)

天花乱坠 tiān huā luàn zhuì

传说梁武帝时，云光法师讲经，感动了天神，天上各种颜色的香花纷纷掉落（坠）下来。形容说话非常动听，但过分夸张，不切实际。例如：有些医生把一些略有减肥效果或根本无减肥效果的药物吹得天花乱坠，这就导致更多的肥胖者盲目尝试，危害到健康。（《中国兴起减肥热》，1991年7月6日《联合早报》第30版）

Making A Wild Boast About Something

Chinese legend had it that during the time of emperor Liang Wu, there was a monk who could preach so movingly that even the Gods were touched and fragrant and colourful flowers of all kinds would drop from the sky. This idiom is nowadays used to describe someone who gives an extravagant account of something.

Example: "Some physicians are 'making a wild boast about' their slimming pills which might have little or no effect at all. Many unsuspecting people were lured into taking them and had their health impaired." (Lianhe Zaobao 6/7/91)

无巧不成书 wú qiǎo bù chéng shū

书：指说书艺人说的长篇故事。这条成语的本义是没有巧合的情节，就不能构成长篇故事。比喻事有凑巧。例如：银行大搞存户幸运抽奖活动。马来亚银行的首奖是一辆宝马牌轿车，所谓无巧不成书，渣打银行也以名贵轿车大打“发达奖”广告，首三奖全是宝马牌轿车。（《送奖派钞，各出奇招》，1991年4月5日《联合早报》第21版）

这条成语原本说成“没巧不成话”或“无巧不成话”，是中国古代说书艺人的口头语；也说成“没巧不成语”或“无巧不成辞”。

Good Stories Are Made Up Of Coincidences

"Shu" here refers to voluminous novels. This Chinese proverb highlights the fact that many interesting stories are inevitable involving various coincidences.

Example: "Many banks are organising lucky draws for their depositors. As the saying goes, 'good stories are made up of coincidences,' Malayan Banking is offering a BMW car as its first prize, while the Standard Chartered Bank is also offering BMW cars for its first three prizes." (Lianhe Zaobao 5/4/91)

想入非非 xiǎng rù fēi fēi

非非：佛家指一般人认识能力所达不到的奥妙而难以捉摸的境界。现在使用这条成语都指胡思乱想或幻想不能实现的事。例如：另两名不愿透露姓名的新航空姐说，"新加坡女郎"不会令人想入非非，我们的沙笼制服根本不算暴露。（《穿沙笼的空姐令人想入非非？》，1991年6月14日《联合早报》第5版）

To Indulge In Fantasy

The term: "Fei Fei" refers originally to a supernatural world in Buddhism which is beyond the imagination of mortals. It is now commonly used to mean a fantasy or an unrealistic desire.

Example: "Two SIA air hostesses said that the 'Singapore Girl' image does not induce others 'to indulge in fantasy', because their uniform does not reveal much of their bodies at all." (Lianhe Zaobao 14/6/91)

小巫见大巫　xiǎo wū jiàn dà wū

巫：以装神弄鬼替人祈祷（qídǎo）为职业的人。小巫是巫师中法术比较低的，大巫是法术高的巫师。小巫师见到了大巫师，就不能施展他的法术了。比喻高下相差很大，不能相比。例如："野村"、"日兴"、"山和"及"山一"也是世界四大证券公司，山姆大叔的同业如跟日本这些大公司相比，也是小巫见大巫。（《日本"泡沫经济"崩溃了》，1991年7月6日《联合早报》第15版）

The Difference Is Too Great For Comparison

Literally, this Chinese proverb means "like a small sorcerer in the presence of a great one". Simply, it means that there is no comparison.

Example: "The four Japanese broking firms are the biggest in the world. Relatively speaking, their counterparts in the US are much smaller. In fact, 'the difference is too great for comparison'." (Lianhe Zaobao 6/7/91)

迅雷不及掩耳　xùn léi bù jí yǎn ěr

迅雷：来得快，震耳欲聋的雷，即通常所谓“炸雷”。全句的意思是，突然响起的雷声使人来不及捂（wǔ）住耳朵，比喻来势迅猛，使人来不及防备。例如：联军以迅雷不及掩耳之势越过沙地伊拉克边界，把伊军包围起来，并切断他们的退路。（《波斯湾战役是西方用兵典范》，1991年3月2日《联合早报》第3版）

这条成语也说成“疾雷不及掩耳”或“捷雷不及掩耳”，也可以减省说成“迅雷不及”。

As Sudden As Lightning

Literally, this Chinese proverb means a sudden peal of thunder leaves no time for covering one's ears. It is used to describe the speed and suddenness of an action or occurrence.

Example: "The Allied troops crossed the Saudi-Iraq borders and advanced 'as suddenly as lightning' to surround the Iraqi army, thus blocking its route of retreat." (Lianhe Zaobao 2/3/91)

养虎为患 yǎng hǔ wéi huàn

为：造成；患：祸害。这个成语的字面意义是：喂养老虎，造成祸害。比喻纵容敌人，给自己造成祸害。例如：海湾危机，是谁养虎为患？（标题，1990年10月15日《联合早报》第11版）

"为"也说"留"、"遗"或"贻"（yí），都当"留下"讲；"患"也说"殃"（yāng）或"灾"，都是"祸害"的意思。

Courting Trouble By Rearing A Tiger

This Chinese idiom is similar in meaning to the English proverb: "Cherishing a serpent in one's bosom". It satirizes a person's indiscreet behaviour which may ultimately bring disaster upon himself.

Example: "The Middle East crisis is threatening the whole world; who indeed has 'courted trouble by rearing a tiger' there?" (Headline in Lianhe Zaobao, 15/10/90)

一板一眼 yī bǎn yī yǎn

板眼：华乐和戏曲中的节拍，每小节中最强的拍子叫板，次强和弱拍叫眼。乐曲节拍有一板一眼，也有一板三眼。因此，一板一眼或一板三眼都是比喻言语、行动有条理，合规矩；也比喻做事死板，不知道变通。

例如：空军总司令卡瑟（kǎsè）最近说，“我们做事要照着泰国方式来做。如果我们根据理论，一板一眼的，我们的民主只会弯弯曲曲的在地上爬”。（《抽刀断水·泰式政变何时了》，1991年4月21日《联合早报》第17版），这个例句中的“一板一眼”用的是上述第二个比喻义。

Following A Prescribed Pattern Scrupulously

“Ban” and “Yan” are rhythmical metres used in Chinese music and operas. “Ban” is a stronger metre whereas “yan” is weaker. This Chinese idiom is used to describe an action that follows the rules very strictly and rigidly.

Example: “Thailand’s air chief marshall said his country must do things according to flexible Thai styles and not ‘to follow prescribed patterns scrupulously’, or else the people would have to crawl on the floor aimlessly.” (Lianhe Zaobao 21/4/91)

一窍不通 yī qiào bù tōng

窍：心窍。比喻一点儿也不懂。例如：其实我对政治一窍不通。我不知道什么叫政治，也不想踏足政治。（《梅艳芳，魔鬼与天使的化身》，1991年5月26日《联合早报》《星期影视》版）

也可以反序说成“不通一窍”。

Knowing Absolutely Nothing

"Qiao" refers to sense of understanding. This Chinese idiom describes someone who does not have the slightest knowledge about a certain subject.

Example: "I 'know absolutely nothing' about politics. I do not know what politics are, and I do not intend to get involved in politics." (Lianhe Zaobao 26/5/91)

一五一十　yī wǔ yī shí

算较大的数目时，常用“五”作为计算的单位往下数，所以“一五一十”原本指计算数目。比喻讲话时从头到尾，原原本本，说得清清楚楚。例如：吴总理希望社区领袖组成类似政府国会委员会的小组，针对比如交通、教育、卫生或国防等课题，征求居民的意见，在他访问时一五一十地加以反映，以发挥“民间议员”的作用。（《多一种语言多一层方便》，1991年6月5日《新明日报》社论）

To Relate In Full Detail

When counting large figures, we usually use “5” or “10” as one unit for easy calculation. This Chinese idiom figuratively describes how an incident or issue is being explained in great detail.

Example: “PM Goh hoped that community leaders could organise committees similar to the GPCs to obtain feedback from residents on issues such as transportation, education, health and defence. They could then ‘relate in full detail’ to him during his visits. This would put into practice the concept of ‘Grassroots Parliament’.” (Shin Min Daily News 5/6/91)

寅吃卯粮 yín chī mǎo liáng

中国的农历以天干、地支纪年。按地支顺序，寅在卯前。寅年吃了卯年的粮食，比喻收入不够支出，预先动用还没有到手的收入。例如：今天的大学毕业生，起薪通常每月就有1400元，他们只需工作三几年，就有资格申请信用卡。但是，这些年轻人会不会量入为出呢？或者是用信用卡寅吃卯粮？所以胡财长的担心并不是没有理由的。（《防止信用卡“满天飞”》，1991年7月6日《联合早报》第14版。量入为出：成语，根据收入来定开支的限度。）

也说“寅支卯粮”。

To Eat Food Reserved For The Next Year

“Yin” and “mao” are two different periods in the lunar calendar year. This Chinese idiom describes a person who is consuming food which has been stored or set aside for a later period. It is used to describe a person who is financially hard up.

Example: “Nowadays, fresh graduates are enjoying a starting salary of $1400 per month. After working for a few years, they are eligible to apply for credit cards. Are they spending more than they are earning? Are they ‘eating food reserved for the next year’? Perhaps, Dr Richard Hu’s worries are not without basis.” (Lianhe Zaobao 6/7/91)

醉翁之意不在酒 zuì wēng zhī yì bù zài jiǔ

“醉翁之意不在酒，在乎山水之间也。”这是中国宋朝欧阳修写的散文《醉翁亭记》里的一句话，意思是真意不在喝酒，而在欣赏山景。这条成语是比喻真实的意图不在这儿，而在别的方面。例如：阿尔巴尼亚共产党内的保守派想把政权再拿到自己的手中来，这激怒了阿尔巴尼亚人。他们走上街头，醉翁之意不在酒，大概不是为了欢迎美国国务卿贝克，而是借机向这些保守派示威吧！（《贝克访阿尔巴尼亚，为什么会受到热烈欢迎？》，1991年6月26日《联合早报》第15版）

这条成语也比喻别有用心，也可以省去“不在酒”三字，说成“醉翁之意”。

The Drinker's Heart Is Not In the Cup

This Chinese proverb was originated from a poem which describes the poet's interest in enjoying the beautiful scenery, and not so much in drinking wine. It is now used figuratively to refer to the ulterior motives of a person.

Example: "The Albanian Communist Party was trying to regain political power and the move deeply angered the people. Under the pretext of welcoming US Secretary of State, James Baker, they took to the streets to demonstrate against the conservatives. Indeed, 'the drinker's heart was not in the cup'!" (Lianhe Zaobao 26/6/91)

折冲尊俎　zhé chōng zūn zǔ

折冲：击退敌军。尊俎：尊，跟"樽"的意思相同，是古代盛酒的器具；俎，祭祀（jìsì）时放肉的器具。

"折冲尊俎"原指在酒席上定下妙计，终于打败敌人取得胜利。也用来指外交谈判。例如：波斯湾危机把冷战后的世界重新拖入战争的泥沼，经过四个多月数十位国家元首的折冲尊俎，终难于避免战争的爆发。（《波斯湾战争打赢了又怎么样？》，1991年1月25日《联合早报》第23版）

这个例句中的"折冲尊俎"是指外交谈判。

To Engage In Diplomatic Negotiations

"Zhe Chong" means to defeat the enemy; "Zun Zu" is wine glasses. This Chinese idiom originally meant to formulate plans to defeat the enemy over glasses of wine. Nowadays, it is commonly used to refer to diplomatic manoeuvres.

Example: "The Gulf crisis has again dragged the post cold-war world into the quagmire of war. More than 10 heads of state have 'engaged in diplomatic negotiations' for over 4 months, but they have eventually failed to avert the war." (Lianhe Zaobao 25/1/91)

八字还没一撇　bā zì hái méi yī piě

"八"字才两画，连起笔的"撇"还没有写出来，哪里谈得上"八"字呢？常用来比喻事情还没有一点影儿。例如：最近娱乐圈内传出一则新闻，说新广演员黄世南和潘玲玲要结婚了，记者向他俩问个究竟，回答是没这回事儿。1991年6月18日《联合早报》副刊《影艺》版在报道这则新闻时，标题是《黄世南、潘玲玲：我们结婚？八字还没一撇呢！》

这条俗语也比喻：（1）打算做某件事，但是还没有动手；（2）事情已经开了头，但是还看不到成功的希望。

"没"也说"没有"或"没见"。

The Character "Eight" Without One Stroke

The Chinese character "八" has only two strokes, so without one stroke, it does not form a complete word at all. This proverb means that there is not the slightest sign of anything happening yet.

Example: "There were rumours that SBC actor Huang Shinan and actress Pan Lingling are getting married. However, when they were asked about it, they both denied it by saying that 'the character eight is still without one stroke'." (Lianhe Zaobao 18/6/91)

兵马未动，粮草先行 bīng mǎ wèi dòng, liángcǎo xiānxíng

兵马：兵士和马匹，指军人；粮草：军用的粮食和草料，指给养（jǐyǎng，部队中需要的物资）。全句的意思是，军队还没有出发，先要准备好足够的物资，供作战的需要。比喻做什么事情，要先有物质准备。例如：兵马未动，粮草先行。美国这次出兵，真的很全面，还未动武，已在波斯湾建立了15座医院，这些野战医院可以动任何手术和提供各种医疗报告。（《美国什锦》，1990年11月23日《联合早报》第21版）

这条俗语中的“兵马”也说成“军马”或“三军”（军队的统称）；前一句也说成“大军未到”，“大军”指人数众多的部队。

Food And Fodder Should Go Before Troops And Horses

Supplies for the soldiers should be despatched and well stocked before their arrival at the war front. This Chinese proverb emphasises the need for proper preparations before embarking on a major venture.

Example: “Indeed, the Americans knew that ‘food and fodder should go before troops and horses’. Even before actual military force is used in the Persian Gulf, they have already built 15 hospitals with full facilities for surgical operations and medical reports.” (Lianhe Zaobao 23/11/90)

不分青红皂白 bù fēn qīng hóng zào bái

青红皂白是四种不同的颜色，皂指黑色。

这条俗语比喻：（1）不管正确错误或有理无理；（2）不问事情的内容和原因；（3）不问是好事还是坏事。

例如：中国最近兴起减肥热，在减肥队伍当中，许多人是不分青红皂白，不问本身肥胖根源，盲目减肥。结果减肥不成，反而严重损害身体健康。（《中国兴起减肥热》，1991年7月6日《联合早报》第30版）。这个例句中的"不问青红皂白"，用的是上述第2个比喻义。

"不分"也说"不问"、"不管"或"哪管"，"青红皂白"也说"青黄皂白"或"皂白"。

To Do Something Indiscriminately

Literally, this Chinese proverb describes someone who "does not differentiate between the colours green, red, black and white" (zao means black). It is used figuratively to describe an action that is committed with total disregard to its causes or consequences.

Example: "There was a craze for slimming in China recently and many people rushed 'to do it indiscriminately' without even trying to find out what were the causes of their obesity. Consequently, instead of having their weight reduced, their health was severely impaired." (Lianhe Zaobao 6/7/91)

不管三七二十一 bùguǎn sān qī èrshí yī

有三个意思：(1)不问是非（正确和错误）情由（情形和原因）；(2)不顾一切；(3)不管怎样，无论如何。

例如：有些肥胖者，不管三七二十一乱服药，结果不但没减轻体重，反而出现头晕、心慌的症状，病情加重。（《中国兴起减肥热》，1991年7月6日《联合早报》第30版）。这个例句中的"不管三七二十一"，用的是上述第一个意思。

"不管"也说"不问"、"不分"、"不理"、"休管"、"哪管"或"管他"；"三七二十一"也说"三七廿一"、"三七念一"或"三七念一，二七十四"。

Regardless Of The Consequences

This Chinese proverb means to act recklessly or to cast all caution aside in order to achieve a certain aim.

Example: "Some obese persons are taking medicine of all kinds 'regardless of the consequences'. As a result, instead of having their weight reduced, they are suffering from various illnesses, such as giddiness, nervousness and other severe symptoms." (Lianhe Zaobao 6/7/91)

不怕慢，只怕站 bù pà màn, zhǐ pà zhàn

“只怕”也说“就怕”或“全怕”。全句的意思是，走路或驾车，慢一点不要紧，就怕停下来不继续前进。

引用这句俗话，常指学习或做事缓慢一些并不要紧，怕的是不去学不去做。言外之意是，只要肯坚持，就一定能成功。例如：讲正确华语在开始时也许不容易，但只要肯用心，“不怕慢，只怕站”，大胆地开口说，耐心学习，自然会把华语学好。（《学讲正确华语・勿夹杂英巫词语》，1990年10月21日《联合早报》第10版）。

这条俗语也说成：“不怕慢，就怕站；站一站，三里半。”后两句的意思是稍微停一下就要落后很长一段路。人们通常只引用前两句。

It's Alright To Be Slow, But Never Stand Still

This Chinese saying means it is better to be late than never.

It is commonly used to encourage slow learners or workers to stick it out and not to give up easily, and that as long as they continue to drive on, they will eventually succeed.

Example: "To learn to speak accurate Mandarin may not be easy initially, nevertheless, 'it's alright to be slow but never stand still', so long as we are diligent and patient, we will be able to master the language." (Lianhe Zaobao 21/10/90)

不知天高地厚 bù zhī tiān gāo dì hòu

有两个意思：（1）不了解事情的严重性或复杂性；（2）形容一个人盲目自满，狂妄无知。

例如：四名不知天高地厚的少年，竟拿血肉之躯开玩笑，他们躺在马路中央，任由汽车从身旁飞驰而过。（《四少年玩死亡游戏，躺公路，挡飞车》，1991年7月8日《新明日报》封面版），这个例句中的"不知天高地厚"，意思是不了解事情的严重性。

这条俗语也说成"不知天有多高，地有多厚"或"不知天高，不知地厚"。

Do Not Know The Immensity Of Heaven And Earth

This Chinese proverb describes someone who does not realise the severity of a situation or tries unrealistically to exaggerate his own abilities.

Example: "Four youths who 'do not know the immensity of heaven and earth', playfully risked their own lives by sleeping in the middle of the road with heavy traffic." (Shin Min Daily News 8/7/91)

吃了秤砣铁了心　chī le chèngtuó tiě le xīn

有条歇后语叫“王八吃秤砣——铁了心”，比喻拿定主意，决不改变。王八：乌龟或鳖（biē）的俗称；秤砣：秤锤，“砣”不要写成“铊”。“吃了秤砣铁了心”是这条歇后语的变体。也说成“吃了秤砣，铁心”、“吃了秤砣死了心”或“吃了秤砣”。

例如：布斯相信，他在伊拉克人侵科威特问题上的判断是对的。一切迹象都显示，他是吃了秤砣铁了心。如有必要，即使有军事、政治危险，他也绝不会退缩，不发动战争。（《美国开战决策机关·白宫五人核心小组》，1991年1月17日《联合早报》第31版）

The Heart Has Hardened As Though Having Swallowed A Metal Weight

This Chinese proverb figuratively describes someone who has already made up his mind and nothing seems to be able to change his decision, and his determination is so firm as though his heart has turned to iron.

Example: “President Bush’s determination to oppose Iraqi invasion of Kuwait is so resolute that ‘his heart has hardened as though he has swallowed a metal weight’. In spite of the political and military risks, he is steadfastly preparing for war.” (Lianhe Zaobao 17/1/91)

出得厅堂，入得厨房　chūde tīngtáng, rùde chúfáng

厅堂：厅，接待客人的地方。厨房：煮饭做菜的屋子。形容女子交际应酬和操持家务样样行，里里外外一把手。例如：这次现代好妻子的竞选条件是，事业有成，有掌握家庭生活的技能，教子有方，家庭和睦，仪表大方，端庄稳重等。既主内，又主外。出得厅堂，入得厨房。（《广东竞选“现代好妻子”》，1991年4月27日《联合早报》第19版）

Be In The Hall Or In The Kitchen, She Is Equally Capable

This Chinese idiom is used commonly to describe a woman who is capable not only of running domestic affairs, but is also skilful in dealing with business outside the home.

Example: "The criteria for selecting the 'Ideal Wife of Today' are that she should be able to maintain a harmonious family, educate the children, behave modestly, and yet is successful in her own career. In other words, whether 'in the hall or in the kitchen, she is equally capable'." (Lianhe Zaobao 27/4/91)

扶不起的阿斗　fúbuqǐ de Ā Dǒu

阿斗：刘备的儿子刘禅（**Liú Shàn**）的小名，为人庸庸碌碌（**yōng yōng lù lù**），没有作为。虽有诸葛亮协助，也未能守住他父亲开创的事业。这条俗语多用来比喻无能的人。例如：落后的设备和管理使得（东德的）工厂成了扶不起的阿斗，关门收摊是唯一出路。（《遥遥无期的美丽新世界——东西德统一后面对诸多问题》，1991年4月24日《联合早报》第17版）

Hopelessly Incompetent

"A Dou" was the infant name of Liu Shan, the son of Liu Bei, one of the kings during China's Three Kingdoms Period. He was incapable and weak, and despite being assisted by Zhuge Liang, the resourceful prime minister, he later lost the kingdom to his rival. His name is now synonymous with weakness and incompetence.

Example: "Out-moded equipment and management methods rendered East German factories 'hopelessly incompetent'. Packing up and closing down is the only way out." (Lianhe Zaobao 24/4/91)

妇女能顶半边天 fùnǚ néng dǐng bànbiāntiān

半边天：原指天空的一部分。因为在现代社会里，妇女的能力与作用跟男子一样大，所以也用来泛指新时代的女性。顶：相当；抵（得上）。

这条俗语的意思是，妇女的能力与作用跟男子一样，没有妇女，许多事情都不好办。例如：妇女能顶半边天！古时候，中国的女性，三步不出闺门（**guīmén**，闺房的门：闺房是从前女子住的内室）；今天，女性不但已经踏出闺门，而且越走越远，准备走遍亚、欧和北美洲。33岁的章秀闱（**wéi**），为了向世人证明男人能做的，女人也做得到，她准备驾车环游世界。（《章秀闱要驾“老爷车”环游世界》，1991年1月7日《联合早报》第2版）

Women Could Shoulder Half The Sky

This is the literal translation of the Chinese saying which indirectly pays tributes to modern women who are now just as capable as their opposite sex.

It also stresses the fact that with the help of women, any task can be accomplished more expediently.

Example: “Indeed, ‘women could now shoulder half the sky’. Unlike their sisters of the past, modern women have not only walked out of the kitchen, but have travelled as far as Europe and North America. Thirty-three year old Zhang Xiuwei is a case in point: she intends to go round the world in her vintage car.” (Lianhe Zaobao 7/1/91)

胳膊扭不过大腿 gēbo niǔbuguò dàtuǐ

胳膊細，大腿粗。比喻地位低的或力量弱的敌不过地位高的或力量强的。例如：据说珠海市对澳门建新机场早就存疑，但是中央说了话，表示同意澳门建机场，投资者中又有中资企业，市长梁广大“胳膊扭不过大腿”。（《广东人难解浦东心意结》，《联合早报》1991年2月12日第27版）

“扭”也说“拧”（nǐng）。这条俗语也说成“脚跟拗不过大腿”或“小腿扭不过大腿”。

The Arm Is No Match For The Thigh

Figuratively, this Chinese proverb means a person who is lower in ranking or weaker in strength cannot win over someone who is higher in position or stronger in physique.

Example: “The City of Zhuhai disagrees with the proposed airport project in Macao, but since the central government has approved of it and Chinese-financed corporations are involved in the venture, Mayor Liang Guangda is helpless, after all ‘an arm is no match for the thigh’.” (Lianhe Zaobao 12/2/91)

各打五十大板 gè dǎ wǔshí dàbǎn

“大板”是中国古代打人的刑具。“打……大板”就是“用大板来打”，意为“责罚”。

“各打五十大板”比喻处理问题不分是非，只是简单地把双方都处罚一顿，表示公正。例如：日本财相桥本龙太郎，以对股市监督不力，以致接连发生“不祥事件”为由，宣布自动减薪10%，为期三个月。他的两名得力助手也受到同样的处分。有人说，财相自己处罚自己很新鲜；也有人说，股票行和监督官各打五十大板，做做样子罢了。（《日本式“指导型”资本主义》，1991年7月14日《联合早报》第2版）

To Blame Both Sides Without Discrimination

“Daban” is a kind of punishment used in ancient China on criminals. This proverb figuratively means to punish the innocent and the guilty alike.

Example: “In the recent financial scandal in Japan, the finance minister offered to cut his own salary by 10%. He also punished his two assistants. However, critics said he was only trying to show that he was ‘blaming both sides without discrimination’.” (Lianhe Zaobao 14/7/91)

狗不嫌主贫，子不嫌母丑

gǒu bù xián zhǔ pín, zǐ bù xián mǔ chǒu

比喻人总是深深地留恋自己的亲人、家庭和故乡。例如：移民后是否要连根拔起，斩断情丝，并尽数原居地种种不是呢？中国俗语云："狗不嫌主贫，子不嫌母丑"。但是，这种文化思想，亦未必人人可以领悟（lǐngwù，领会）。（《新人谈故人》，1991年4月21日《联合早报》第2版）

这条俗语也说成"狗不嫌家贫，人不嫌地薄"，或"狗不舍穷家"。

Anything Near Is Always Dear

Literally, this Chinese saying means a dog would not resent its master because he is poor; nor would a son dislike his mother because she is ugly. Figuratively, it means people always feel close to their family members and native land, however imperfect they may be.

Example: "Should a migrant remark disparagingly about his native land after severing their ties with it? As the Chinese saying goes 'Anything near is always dear', unfortunately, not everybody appreciates such cultural affinities." (Lianhe Zaobao 21/4/91)

黑猫白猫，能捉老鼠就是好猫

hēi māo bái māo, néng zhuō lǎoshǔ jiù shì hǎo māo

比喻做事重在看效果。例如："不管黑猫白猫，能捉老鼠的就是好猫"，不管你说坏还是叫好，能打开商品销路的就是好广告！（《刀锋骇（hài）人，鲜血直滴/受议论广告·汽车销路直上》，1990年10月30日《联合晚报》第2版）

这条俗语也说成"不管黄猫花猫，抓住老鼠就是好猫"，"不管黑猫白猫，抓着耗子的就是好猫"或"不管黄牛黑牛，能拉犁的就是好牛"。

Be It A Black Cat Or A White Cat, As Long As It Catches Mice, It Is A Good Cat

This Chinese saying stresses the irrelevance of appearance and the importance of practical value.

It is similar in meaning to a comment in Lianhe Wanbao on 30/10/90 about the controversial Mitsubishi car advertisement when it said, "Be it pleasant or unpleasant, as long as it boosts sales, it is a good ad."

虎父无犬子 hǔ fù wú quǎn zǐ

比喻有本事的父亲，不会养育出无能的儿子，意即上一代强，下一代不会弱。例如：新秀组的两个荣誉奖，由罗云诺和占米诺兄弟俩夺得，他们是抽象画组冠军班柯鲁斯的儿子，真可称得上“虎父无犬子”。（《大华银行集团主办的绘画比赛，成绩昨天揭晓》，1991年7月4日《联合早报》第3版）。

Like Father Like Son

Literally, this Chinese proverb means "If the father is like a tiger, his son cannot be like a dog." It is used to describe the son who is more capable than his father.

Example: "In the UOB Art Competition, the two distinction prizes were won by two brothers, Lovina and Jamilo de Cruz. Their father, Ben de Cruz also won the first prize in the Abstract Painting Section. It is indeed 'like father like sons'." (4/7/91)

花无百日红　huā wú bǎi rì hóng

花开了总有谢的时候，不可能长开不败。这条俗语比喻事情总会起变化，不可能永远那么理想。例如：新加坡自建国以来，经济发展迅速、蓬勃……但是，正所谓“花无百日红”，碰上全球性不景气，新加坡的经济，在1985年出现衰退的迹象。（《增加公积金就是加薪》，1991年3月13日《新明日报》社论）

这条俗语常跟“人无千日好”连用，说成“人无千日好，花无百日红”，或倒过来说成“花无百日红，人无千日好”。“花无百日红”也说成“花无百日开”或“花无百日好”。

跟这条俗语同义的还有“花无长红，月无常圆”。

All Good Things Never Last Forever

Literally, this Chinese proverb means all flowers will not stay in full bloom for a hundred days.

It is used figuratively to emphasise the fact that nothing in life can remain flourishing and unchanging for very long.

Example: “Since independence, Singapore has achieved rapid economic development and prosperity, but as ‘all good things never last forever’, the country showed signs of the decline during the global economic recession in 1985.” (Shin Min Daily News 13/3/91)

鸡蛋里挑骨头 jīdànli tiāo gǔtou

比喻故意挑剔毛病（挑剔：tiāoti，过分严格地在細节上挑出错误，加以批评）。例如：看到自己的姓名以本民族的文字印在身分证上，谁都会有一份喜悦和亲切感，虽然小部分唱反调的会说："姓名印在照片之下，简直就像通缉犯。"我倒觉得那未免是鸡蛋里挑骨头。（《大受欢迎的措施》，1991年6月6日《新明日报》第8版）。

"挑骨头"也说"找骨头"或"寻出骨头"。

To Look For A Bone In An Egg

It means to look for flaw where there is none or to find fault deliberately.

Example: "It gives me much pleasure and a sense of familiarity to see my own Chinese name on the Identity Card, although some people disagreed and said it made them look like wanted persons, I think they were trying 'to look for a bone in an egg'." (Shin Min Daily News 6/6/91)

江山易改，本性难移 jiāng shān yì gǎi, běnxìng nán yí

江山：河流与山岳；本性：个性、性格；移：改变。这条俗语的意思是，山岳河流容易改变，一个人的个性很难改变。例如：华族的另外一个特殊性格就是服从……从古至今是如此，未来也是如此，所谓江山易改，本性难移，这句俗语用来形容华族性格，妙不可言。（《中国人的民族性》，1991年6月23日《联合早报》第2版。妙不可言：成语，美妙到了极点，无法用语言表达。）

“江山”也说成“山河”；“易改”也说成“可改”或“好改”；“本性”也说成“禀性”或“秉性”（禀、秉：bǐng）。这条俗语也说成“山河容易改，本性最难移”或“本性难移，山河易改”。

It's Easy To Change The Rivers And Mountains, But Hard To Change A Person's Nature

This Chinese idiom is similar in meaning to the English proverb: "The leopard cannot change its spots".

Example: "A national trait of the Chinese people is their submissiveness to absolute authority. . . This has always been so from time immemorial. The idiom: 'It's easy to change rivers and mountains, but hard to change a person's nature' can very aptly be used to describe this characteristic." (Lianhe Zaobao 23/6/91)

巾帼不让须眉 jīnguó bù ràng xūméi

巾帼：中国古代妇女用的头巾和发饰，借指妇女。让：退让、让步。须眉：胡须和眉毛。中国古代以男子浓眉密须为美，所以用须眉来代替男子汉大丈夫。

巾帼不让须眉常用来指在竞争或比赛等情况下，妇女不会向男子退让或让步。言外之意是妇女跟男子一样有能耐。例如：巾帼不让须眉·21女性候选人角逐13国8州（标题，1990年10月15日《联合早报》第8版）。

Women Are As Good As Men

"Jinguo" is a kind of ancient women's headdress. It is used to refer to women in general. Similarly, "Xumei", which means beard and eye-brows refers specifically to men. This Chinese adage stresses that in a particular contest or competition, the female participants are showing equally impressive performances as their male counterparts.

Example: "In the coming general elections, 21 female candidates are contesting 13 parliamentary and 8 state assembly seats, indeed, 'women are as good as men'." (Lianhe Zaobao 15/10/90)

九牛二虎之力 jiǔ niú èr hǔ zhī lì

九头牛和两只老虎的力气。比喻很大的气力或很大的力量。例如：学校图书馆虽有华文书籍，但华文教师须花九牛二虎之力，才能把一部分学生引上阅读华文书报的道路。（《华文文学往哪里去？》，1991年7月5日《联合早报》第16版）

The Strength Of Nine Bulls And Two Tigers

The Chinese proverb is commonly used to describe the extraordinary strength or effort put in by a person.

Example: "Although the library has many Chinese books, the Chinese teachers have to use 'the strength of nine bulls and two tigers' to get some students to read them regularly." (5/7/91)

烂船三斤钉 làn chuán sān jīn dīng

烂：破烂；船：指木船。比喻有钱的人家即使衰落了，也还有些家底儿（家底儿：jiādǐr，家里长期累积起来的财产）。例如：法国《解放报》社论剖析说：苏联国势是大不如前了；然而“烂船三斤钉”，戈尔巴乔夫还有能力开展一场“外交威慑”（威慑：wēishè，用武力使对方感到恐惧），使美国不能自信稳操胜券，也就是白宫还得 (děi) 有求于他。（《苏联在战争中扮演的角色》，1991年2月19日《联合早报》第25版。“稳操胜券”：成语，比喻有充分的把握。）

这条俗语也说成：“船烂还有三千钉”，“大船烂了还有三千个钉”，“烂船有三斤钉”，“烂船拾起有三斤钉”，或“破船还有三千钉”等。

A Worn-Out Boat Has Many Nails

"Jin" is a unit of weight. Here it means "many".

This Chinese proverb is used figuratively to illustrate the fact that a very rich family even after it has declined in wealth, would still have considerable assets to fall back on. It is also used in a similar sense to describe a nation which has declined in power.

Example: "Although the Soviet Union's political position has diminished substantially, Mr Gorbachev can still wield much diplomatic influence to ensure his country remains a force to be reckoned with, especially in its dealings with the US. After all, 'a worn-out boat still has many nails'." (Lianhe Zaobao 19/2/91)

老鹰捉小鸡　lǎoyīng zhuō xiǎo jī

形容动作又轻又猛，又狠又准，用不着费多大气力，事情就成功了。例如：我们相信，美军的战略决不会是老老实实的强攻科威特，也不会和驻在科威特北部的十五万共和国卫队精兵正面交锋。它多半是向伊拉克中部发动攻击，伊军如北上迎战，美国空军就在空中发动老鹰捉鸡式的攻击。那也是用己所长，攻敌所短。（《猪木斗阿里，硬不起身》（时事漫谈），1991年1月25日《联合早报》第22版）

Eagle Swooping Down Upon The Chick

This is the direct translation of the Chinese proverb which describes a job that is easy yet extremely vigorous and effective.

Example: "We believe that the American strategy is not to straight-forwardly attack the Iraqis, nor will it directly clash with the Republican Guard stationed in northern Kuwait. It is more likely to raid central Iraq and uses its air force to bombard the Iraqi soldiers, just like the 'eagle swooping down upon the chicks', thus taking advantage of the enemy's weaknesses". (Lianhe Zaobao 25/1/91)

两条腿走路 liǎng tiáo tuǐ zǒu lù

比喻在做某一件事的时候应照顾到两方面。例如：有人说，圣公会中学的学业成绩优异，要读好学校，就选圣公会。另一些人则认为，圣公会的体育最出色，有这方面天分的学生可以选读。其实，圣公会奉行的是“两条腿政策”——体育与学业并重。（《圣公会中学，两条腿走路》，1991年5月24日《联合早报》第33版）

这条俗语也比喻在做某一件事时，同时采用两种方法。

To Walk On Two Legs

This Chinese idiom refers to a two-pronged policy that places equal emphasis on two aspects of development, especially in the field of economy or education.

Example: “Some people said that the St Anglican is a good school, particularly for students who want to excel in sports. Actually, the school is ‘walking on two legs’ — putting equal emphasis on sports and studies.” (Lianhe Zaobao 24/5/91)

萝卜白菜，各有所爱 luóbo báicài, gè yǒu suǒ ài

比喻各人有各人的胃口。例如：北京市现有百岁以上的老人40位，其中37位女性，3位男性。在饮食习惯上，这些老寿星是"萝卜白菜，各有所爱"。他们大多不喜烟酒，但有的对烟酒持"拿来主义"。有的吃素不吃荤，有的喜甜不喜咸。（《北京人瑞40名・女性有37人》，1990年12月15日《联合晚报》第16版）

这条俗语有时比喻人各有志。

Radish Or Cabbage, Everybody Has His Own Preference

This Chinese saying stresses the fact that people tend to have their own peculiar preferences in eating and do not necessarily share a common taste.

Example: "There are 40 centenarians in Beijing City, 37 of them female and 3 male. When it comes to eating, 'radish or cabbage, each has his own preference'; some are vegetarians others are not, some like sweet things others prefer more salty stuff. Generally, they do not drink and smoke unless they are offered free on specific occasions." (Lianhe Wanbao 15/12/90)

麻雀虽小，五脏俱全 máquè suī xiǎo, wǔzàng jùquán

五脏：心、肝、脾（pí）、肺和肾；俱全：齐全。比喻事物虽小，其中各个部分却都齐全。例如：浦东也积极发展成为一个“麻雀虽小，五脏俱全”的金融银行区，允许外资银行设立分行及财务机构。（《浦东投资前景仍待观察》，1991年5月14日《联合早报》社论）。

这条俗语的后一小句也说成“肝胆俱全”。

Small But Complete

Literally, this Chinese proverb means the sparrow may be small but it has all the vital organs. “Wuzang” refers to heart, liver, spleen, lung and kidney.

Example: “Pudong (in Shanghai) is developing a financial centre which will be ‘small but complete’. It will allow foreign banks to set up branches and financial offices.” (Lianhe Zaobao 14/5/91)

漫天要价，就地还钱　màntiān yàojià, jiùdì huán qián

漫天：形容没有边际或没有限度，这里指非常高。要价：说出货物的售价。就地：本指就在原处，这里形容非常低。还钱：还价，不是本地常用的“付钱”的意思。

全句的意思是，卖方把售价开得很高，买方却把价钱还得很低。例如：我们很快地发现，意大利的摊贩喜欢漫天要价，顾客可以就地还钱。大家喜出望外，一路上压抑（yì）着的杀价潜能，顿时得到了施展的机会。（《意大利去来》，1990年10月25日《联合早报》《茶馆》版）

这条俗语也说成“上天要价，落地还钱”，而前一句也说成“满天要价”、“满天开价”、“漫天开价”或“瞒天讨价”。

To Ask For A Sky-High Price, To Pay An On-The-Spot Sum

This is the literal translation of the Chinese saying. It illustrates a lively trading scene at which the sellers and buyers are bargaining for outrageous prices.

Example: “We soon found out that the Italian street sellers always ‘asked for sky-high prices, but buyers could pay an on-the-spot sum’. Everyone was overjoyed at the opportunity: their long-suppressed instinct for bargaining could now be given a full rein.” (Lianhe Zaobao 25/10/90)

摸着石头过河　mōzhe shítou guò hé

摸着河里的石头过河，一步踩（cǎi）稳了，再迈（mài，抬腿跨出）一步。比喻做事要稳妥（wěntuǒ，稳当可靠），一步一步地前进。例如：日列夫总统说："走市场经济道路并不很容易，会遇到很多困难。"我问他："中国有句俗语，叫摸着石头过河，保加利亚目前也是处于这种情况吗？"日列夫回答道："我不太懂这句话的含义，不过中国的改革经验，很值得我们学习和研究。"（《总统夫人第一个失业——在餐桌上访保加利亚总统》，1991年5月9日《联合早报》第15版）

"摸着"也说"摸到"；这条俗语后边也可以再接一个小句，说成"摸着石头过河，踩稳一步再迈一步"。

To Cross The River By Feeling The Stones

To cross the river step by step with the support of the stones. This Chinese proverb figuratively describes how a person carries out a job with great caution.

Example: "I asked the president of Bulgaria whether the way his country developed its market economy was like 'crossing the river by feeling the stones', he replied by saying that China's experience in economic reform indeed deserves close study and emulation." (Lianhe Zaobao 9/5/91)

碰了一鼻子灰 pèngle yī bízi huī

比喻本想讨好，结果遭到拒绝或斥责，落了个没趣。例如：耶特辛趁戈尔巴乔夫去东京访问时也来到西欧，本想得到各国的支持，在议会上好好捞上一票，谁知碰了一鼻子灰。（《苏联的局势能缓和吗？》，1991年5月10日《联合早报》第19版）

"碰"也说"抹"、"咂"（zá）、"撞"、"吃"、"弄"或"臊"（sào），"了"字可省。

To Meet With A Rebuff

This Chinese saying describes how a person is rudely snubbed while trying to please others. Literally it means to have one's nose covered with dust after banging against the wall.

Example: "Yeltsin took the opportunity to visit Western Europe while Gorbachev was in Tokyo. He was trying to win the support of these countries but was instead 'met with a rebuff'." (Lianhe Zaobao 10/5/91)

千军易得，一将难求 qiān jūn yì dé, yī jiàng nán qiú

征集成千的兵士倒容易，寻求一个好的将领却很困难。比喻人才难得。例如：千军易得，一将难求。我相信，中共在长征途中，一定会以保全毛泽东、周恩来、任弼时、刘少奇、刘伯承等高级指挥人员的性命为优先考虑。同样的道理，为国家民族计，重视知识分子当为第一要务。（《中国经改过程所应注意的几个问题》，1991年6月4日《联合早报》第14版）

也说成“三军易得，一将难求”，“千兵易得，一将难求”，“千军容易得，一将最难求”或“要得千军易，偏求一将难”。

It's Easy To Raise An Army, But Difficult To Get A Good General

This Chinese proverb stresses the fact that talented people do not come by easily.

Example: "The Chinese Communist Party should know that 'it's easy to raise an army, but difficult to get a good general'. I am sure that during the Long March, it took extra care to protect its leaders. For the sake of China's future it should now take good care of its intellectuals." (Lianhe Zaobao 4/6/91)

牵着鼻子走 qiānzhe bízi zou

像牛一样被人牵着，比喻被人所控制。例如：我觉得我是一个艺人，我要带领一个潮流，我不喜欢别人牵着我的鼻子走。（《梅艳芳，魔鬼与天使的化身》，1991年5月26日《联合早报》《星期影视》版）

也说成“牵了鼻子走”或“牵着鼻子”。

To Be Led By The Nose

Figuratively, it describes someone who is being led along by others like an ox.

Example: “I feel that as an artiste, I should initiate a new trend by myself, rather than ‘to be led by the nose’ by others.” (Lianhe Zaobao 26/5/91)

人靠衣装，佛要金装 rén kào yī zhuāng, fó yào jīn zhuāng

人要靠衣服装扮，佛像要靠金粉来修饰，指服饰打扮，对人的仪表有很大的作用。例如：“人靠衣装，佛要金装”。前些日子，张敏穿上一件性感的露肩裙子，更散发出动人的风韵。（《张敏每年花15万买衣服》，1991年7月6日《联合早报》《影艺》版。）

也说成“佛是金装，人是衣装”或“佛要金装，人要衣装”。

Dresses Make The Person

Literally, this Chinese proverb means “people have to dress up properly to create a good impression, while an Buddhist idol needs golden paint to look respectable”.

Example: “Recently, when actress Zhan Min wore a low-cut sexy dress, she looked radiantly attractive. Indeed, ‘dresses make the person’.” (6/7/91)

人怕出名猪怕肥 rén pà chūmíng zhū pà féi

猪长肥了就会被宰杀，供人享用：人一出名，往往会招来许多不必要的麻烦。例如：正所谓“人怕出名猪怕肥”。“多金”给张荣发（台湾长荣集团创办人）带来的不只是“出名”，更糟的是把它抬上社会新闻的头条。1989年11月17日，他的第二个儿子张国明被绑架，绑匪勒索赎金新台币5000万元（约新币312万元）。（《两名保镖随身，住家挖神秘地道》，1991年7月2日《新明日报》第6版）

“肥”也说“壮”。

Fame Portends Trouble For Men Just As Fattening Does For Pigs

When the pigs are fat enough, they will be sent for slaughtering; similarly, when people are too famous, they may invite troubles.

Example: “Taiwanese tycoon Cheng Rong Fatt was widely known for his wealth, but he had also met with many troubles. In 1989, his second son was abducted and the kidnappers demanded as much as NT$50 million. Indeed, ‘fame portends trouble for men just as fattening does for pigs’.” (Shin Min Daily News 2/7/91)

大意失荆州 dàyi shī Jīngzhōu

荆州：中国古代地名，今湖北省江陵县。三国时代（公元220—280年），荆州是蜀（Shǔ）国政治军事重镇。据《三国演义》描写，镇守荆州的关羽看不起东吴的孙权，当他出兵攻打曹操的时候，荆州没有严密设防，于是孙权乘机派兵袭取荆州，关羽被捉。这句俗话是比喻疏忽大意，造成重大错误。例如：沈殿霞这一回真个是大意失荆州。为了贪图凉快，整日躲在酒店的冷气房间里睡觉，让郑少秋独自在外拍片，使他有机会追求官晶华。官晶华明知郑少秋已有亲密女友，照样跟秋官勾搭，横刀夺爱。（《沈殿霞大意失荆州·郑少秋别恋官晶华》，1990年10月29日、30日《联合晚报》《歌影视》版）

Losing Jingzhou As A Result Of An Oversight

"Jingzhou" was a city in ancient China. When Guan Yu, the renowned Chinese general was its military commander during the Three-Kingdom Period, he left it insufficiently defended when he led the army to fight Cao Cao, his greatest adversary, the city was unexpectedly overrun by Sun Quan, another rival.

This proverb describes how a minor negligence can lead to a serious error.

Example: "Hongkong film star Lydia Sum enjoyed the comfort of the hotel and left her actor husband behind at the studio, he later fell in love with another girl. Lydia ended up 'losing Jingzhou as a result of an oversight'." (Lianhe Wanbao 29/10/90)

狮子大开口 shīzi dà kāikǒu

上海话词语。有两个意思：（1）说大话；（2）要求高，胃口大。例如：西方国家的政治领袖们并没有觉得戈尔巴乔夫是狮子大开口，而是当真研究起千亿美元援苏计划的可行性。（《乌龙翻译误导出的千亿美元援苏案》，1991年5月28日《联合早报》第14版）。这句话里的"狮子大开口"，用的是上述第二个意思。

To Ask For The Sky

This Chinese saying is a Shanghainese dialect which literally means the lion opens its mouth widely. It figuratively describes someone who is boasting or asking for an incredibly huge sum of money.

Example: "Leaders of western countries do not think that Mr Gorbachev is 'asking for the sky', and are seriously studying the feasibility of the US$100 billion aid programme." (Lianhe Zaobao 28/5/91)

瘦死的骆驼比马肥 shòu sǐ de luòtuo bǐ mǎ féi

比喻有钱有势人家，即使衰落了，也比一般人家强。也比喻某种势力虽然已经衰落下来，但也不能小看。例如：停战后，即使伊拉克在短期内无法再对外动武，一时难以再侵略邻国，但是美国仍然认为“瘦死的骆驼比马肥”，伊拉克残余的军力仍可名列中东强国之林。（《美国怎能不除掉胡申》，1991年2月23日《联合早报》第13版）。这个例句中的“瘦死的骆驼比马肥”，应照上述第二个比喻义来理解。

“肥”一般都说成“大”。跟这条俗语同义的还有“瘦骆驼强似象”和“瘦骆驼尚有千斤肉”。

A Thin Camel Is Fatter Than A Horse

This is a literal translation of the Chinese saying which figuratively means a rich and powerful family even after experiencing a setback is still wealthier than an average family. It can also be similarly used to describe a defeated nation.

Example: “After the ceasefire, Iraq may not be able to adopt an aggressive posture and threaten its neighbours in the near future, but the US seems to believe that ‘a thin camel is fatter than a horse’, as Iraq’s remaining military strength might still make it a superpower in the Middle East.” (Lianhe Zaobao 23/2/91)

树大有枯枝　shù dà yǒu kū zhī

比喻聚集的人多了，当中免不了有少数坏人。例如：郑太太说，她买房子的时候也险些被经纪欺骗，使她不开心了一阵子。不过，她们（指一批来自香港的家庭主妇）觉得，"树大有枯枝"是难免的了。总的来说，新加坡人还是热心助人的。（《"41号大酒店"里的小故事》，1991年6月8日《联合早报》第7版）

There Is A Black Sheep In Every Flock

Literally, this Chinese proverb means there is a withered twig in every big tree. Meaning there are bound to be bad hats in any society.

Example: "Mrs Zheng said she was almost cheated by a broker when she bought her house recently. As a Hongkonger, she felt that Singaporeans are generally helpful, nevertheless, 'there is a black sheep in every flock'." (Lianhe Zaobao 8/6/91)

顺得哥情失嫂意 shùnde gē qíng shī sǎo yì

比喻依了这个人，那个人不满意。例如：尤其像我们这样的多元种族、多元语文的社会，政府的政策有时难免顾此失彼，顺得哥情失嫂意。（《“公民社会”的真谛》，1991年6月23日《联合早报》第2版。顾此失彼：成语，顾了这个，丢了那个。真谛：zhēndì，真实意义或道理。）

也说成“顺得姑来失嫂意”。

It's Difficult To Please Everyone

Literally, this Chinese proverb means to listen to my brother would surely offend my sister-in-law, it stresses the fact that it's impossible to always make everybody happy.

Example: "In our multi-racial, multi-lingual society especially, it's often impossible for government policy to take care of all interests. After all, 'it's difficult to please everyone'." (Lianhe Zaobao 23/6/91)

同行是冤家 tónghánq shì yuānjia

同行：同行业的人。冤家：仇人；同一行业的人，因为利害冲突，所以互相妒忌（dùjì）、互相排挤，好像仇人一样。例如：新凤霞指出，“同行是冤家”这种心态，以江青最为典型。（《“她早就该死！”》，1991年6月6日《新明日报》第2版）

People Of The Same Occupation Are Competitors

People in the same business or occupation, due to conflict of interest, may sometimes harbour enmity against each other.

Example: “A former actress who was a victim of the Cultural Revolution said that Jiang Qing hated her because ‘people of the same occupation are competitors’.” (Shin Min Daily News 6/6/91)

兔子不吃窝边草 tùzi bù chī wō biān cǎo

据说兔子为了掩蔽自己，不吃窝旁边的青草。比喻坏人不在家门口或当地干坏事，也比喻不去侵犯自己周围人的利益。例如：据说这些卖艺的，确实有偷盗的情况，多半是因为实在活不下去了。但是，兔子不吃窝边草，他们是有计划地选择目标。（《响马不吃窝边草》，1991年4月29日《联合早报》第19版。响马：xiǎng mǎ，强盗。）

“兔子”也说“兔儿”或“狡兔”，“不吃”也说“不食”或“弗（fú，不）食”，“窝”也说“窠”（kē，鸟兽的窠穴）。

跟这条俗语同义的有“老鹰不吃窝下食”和“猛虎不吃傍窝食”（傍窝食：窝近旁的食物）。

The Rabbit Would Not Eat The Grass Around Its Burrow

It is said that the rabbits normally would not eat the grass surrounding the burrow which helps to conceal them from the enemy.

Figuratively, it means that even criminals would not commit crimes in their own neighbourhood for fear of hurting their own interests.

Example: “It is true that these street performers did commit crimes at times, that was when they were really hard pressed. After all, ‘the rabbit would not eat the grass around its burrow,’ they normally chose their targets very carefully.” (Lianhe Wanbao 29/4/91)

外来的和尚会念经　wàilái de héshang huì niànjīng

外来：这里指外地。这条俗语比喻迷信从外地来的人才。例如：也许基于"外来的和尚会念经"的心理，有的雇主甚至对外籍雇员另眼相看，而冷落本国同胞。（《新人、敌人、新加坡人》，1991年3月31日《联合早报》第2版）

这条俗语中的"的"字可省，"外来"也说"远来"，"会念经"也说"好看经"。

Foreign Monks Can Chant The Scriptures Better

This is the literal translation of the Chinese proverb which satirizes those people who believe that foreigners are always more capable.

Example: "Perhaps due to the misconception that 'foreign monks can chant the scriptures better', some local employers treat their foreign workers exceptionally well and do not value their own fellow citizens." (Lianhe Zaobao 31/3/91)

万贯家财，不如一技藏身 wànguàn jiā cái, bùrú yī jì cángshēn

万贯：古代的铜钱中间有孔，用来穿钱的绳索叫贯。一千钱叫一贯，万贯是形容钱很多。家财：家产。技：本领、专长。这句俗语的意思是家产再多，不如掌握一门技术（或本领、专长）。言外之意是家产再多，也会坐吃山空，有一技之长，到哪里都可以谋生，强调技术重要。“藏”也说“旁”（读bàng）或“傍”，都当“依附”讲。

例如：俗语说：万贯家财，不如一技藏身，尤其对学历不高的男女来说，这句话更是至理名言。（《�芳自得之余回馈社会》，1990年10月9日《新明日报》第10版）。

跟这条俗语意思相同的还有：“家有千金，不如薄艺随身”、“积财千万，不如薄技在身”。

A Useful Skill Is Better Than Huge Family Fortune

"Guan" is a type of coin used in ancient China. Thousands of "guan" means a huge fortune.

This Chinese proverb stresses the need to acquire a good skill for earning a livelihood, even if one's family is rich. Reason: a fortune, however large, can be squandered, whereas a useful skill is a surer guarantee of survival in the long run.

Example: "It is said that a useful skill is better than a huge family fortune, this is particularly true for men and women who possess no high qualifications." (Shin Min Daily News 9/10/90)

五百年前是一家 wǔ bǎi nián qián shì yī jiā

五百年前本是一家人。同姓的人见面，常讲这句话，目的是拉攀(lāpān)关系，表示祖先是同一宗族。例如：我姓张，汉卿（Hànqīng，即张学良）将军可以说是我的同宗，当然，这是指五百年前是一家的同宗关系了。（张从兴：《为张学良将军鸣不平》，1991年5月21日《联合早报》第19版），这句话里的“五百年前是一家”仅表示，作者跟张学良同姓。

这条俗语也可以用来表示：(1)亲戚关系远得很；(2)关系密切（含诙谐【huīxié】幽默〔humour〕义）。

这条俗语也说成“五百年前共一家”。

Belonging To The Same Family 500 Years Ago

The Chinese believe that those who share the same surname have actually descended from the same family many years ago. The term is sometimes used in a humorous sense to associate oneself with another who has the same surname.

Example: “My surname is Zhang, same as General Zhang Xueliang. We belong to the same family 500 years ago.” (Lianhe Zaobao 21/5/91)

羊毛出在羊身上 yángmáo chū zài yáng shēnshang

羊毛是从羊身上剪下来的。比喻给对方的钱或物，原是从对方取来的，也指把各种负担转嫁给别人（转嫁：zhuǎnjià，把自己应当承受的负担、损失等，加在别人身上）。

例如：在吴总理访问社区时，几乎每一区的商联会代表都表示，担心日后买不起经营已久的店铺。另一个令人忧虑的问题是“羊毛出在羊身上”。如果店屋售价过高，最后消费人的负担也会加重。（《丹那的“小葫芦”》，1991年6月29日《联合早报》第8版），在这个例句中，“羊毛出在羊身上”指的是“把各种负担转嫁给别人”。

The Wool Still Has To Come From The Sheep's Back

This Chinese proverb means that whatever benefit one gets, he may still have to pay back in the end, perhaps in a different form.

Example: "Almost all the representatives of the Singapore Merchants' Association told PM Goh during his recent walkabout that they were worried about their financial capabilities to purchase their shophouses. Some residents expressed the worry that 'the wool may still have to come from the sheep's back': the high cost of shophouses may be passed down to the consumers eventually." (Lianhe Zaobao 29/6/91)

一表三千里 yī biǎo sān qiān lǐ

表：表亲；三千里，形容地域宽广。这条俗语是形容亲属中表亲最多，分布地域最广，甚至难以算清。例如：这个爷爷、那个奶奶，虽然没有中国"一表三千里"那么复杂，但也够说一气的。(《"难道一点对的都没有？"——统一后的前东德近况》，1991年4月2日《联合早报》第14版)

这条俗语后边还可以加一个小句："表到哪里算哪里"。

Relatives Spread Over Three Thousand Miles

"Biao" means relatives, particularly cousins. This Chinese proverb is used to describe one who has very wide family connections.

Example: "This is my grandpa, that is my grandma; although I may not have 'relatives spread over three thousand miles' as people in China, it is nevertheless big enough." (Lianhe Zaobao 2/4/91)

一夜夫妻百日恩 yī yè fūqī bǎi rì ēn

形容一旦结为夫妻，深厚的感情经过很长的时间都不会减退。例如：有人写信到报馆要求杯葛郑少秋，沈殿霞听说后表示非常感谢观众的支持。不过，她希望观众不要杯葛秋仔，因为一夜夫妻百日恩，虽然跟秋仔分开了，但也不愿看到他出什么问题。（《一夜夫妻百日恩·肥肥请观众支持秋仔》，1990年11月25日《联合晚报》第16版）

这句俗话也说成“一夜夫妻百夜恩”、“一日夫妻百日恩”、“一夜夫妻百夜情”、“一夜夫妻，百日恩义”或“一日夫妻，百日恩情”。也可以加一句说成“一日夫妻百日恩，百日夫妻似海深”或“一日夫妻百日恩，百日夫妻一辈子亲”：都形容夫妻感情十分深厚。

Once Committed As Husband And Wife Indebted To Each Other For Life

This Chinese proverb stresses the strong bond between husband and wife. Once committed in marriage, their feelings for each other would last for a very long time.

Example: “Actress Lydia Sum thanked her fans for their support, but urged them not to boycott her ex-husband, actor Cheng Siew Chow because ‘once committed as husband and wife, indebted to each other for life’; although now separated, she didn’t want to see him in trouble.” (Lianhe Wanbao 25/11/90)

英雄出少年 yīngxióng chū shàonián

少年：这里指一般的年轻人。这条俗语的意思是：杰出的人物多从年轻人当中涌现。

跆拳道运动已成为联络所开办的体育活动班级中，最受欢迎的项目。布莱德岭联络所的跆拳道班，目前有学员80人，年龄从5岁到25岁。《联合早报》在报道这个联络所的跆拳道活动时，新闻的标题是“英雄出少年”。（1991年6月30日《联合早报》第19版）

“出少年”也说成“出于”或“出在”。

Heroes Emerge From Among The Youths

This Chinese proverb stresses the fact that those who show outstanding qualities are usually found among the young people.

In a report describing the enthusiastic response to a taekwando course organised by the Braddell Heights Community Centre in which the trainees are all young people between the age of 5 to 25, the Lianhe Zaobao headlined: “Heroes emerge from among the youths.” (30/6/91)

英雄所见略同 yīngxióng suǒ jiàn lüè tóng

所见：这里指见解；略同：大致相同。指杰出人物的见解大致相同，常用来赞美观点、意见相同的几方。例如：我们更不能忘记，不管英文有多重要，有多方便，我们毕竟不是一个西方国家。在这个问题上，李资政与吴总理都有着英雄所见略同的看法。（《根据多数人的愿望来作决定》，1991年6月4日《联合早报》社论）

也说“智者所见略同”或“英雄所见，毕竟略同”。

Great Minds Think Alike

Literally, this Chinese proverb means the views of heroes are basically the same.

It is used commonly as a compliment to people who share similarly brilliant ideas.

Example: “We must not forget that although English is important and convenient, we are after all not a western country. In this aspect, PM Goh and Senior Minister Lee share the same views. ‘Great minds really think alike’.” (Lianhe Zaobao 4/6/91)

有一说一　yǒu yī shuō yī

指说话老老实实，没有虚假的成分。例如：当天的座谈会最大的特点是，讲话的人直爽、真诚，朱镕基更是反应快，思想敏捷。德国商会主席说，今天的讨论会如此成功，是因为以朱镕基先生为首的上海代表团有一说一，坦率、真诚。（《朱镕基在汉堡印象记》，1991年5月4日《联合早报》第13版）

这条俗语也可以再加一句说成"有一说一，有二说二"或"有一说一，有二话二"，还可以说成"有一句说一句"。

Always Says What He Means

This Chinese idiom describes a person who is totally candid and straightforward.

Example: "All the speakers at the forum were frank and sincere. Mr Zhu Rongji's reaction to questions from the audience was swift and intelligent. The president of the German Chamber of Commerce said the success of the forum was due to Mr Zhu's frankness, who 'always said what he meant'." (Lianhe Zaobao 4/5/91)

冤家路窄，狭路相逢 yuānjia lù zhǎi, xiálù xiāng féng

冤家：仇人或不愿相见的人；窄、狭：同义，都指宽度小；相逢：彼此见面。

全句的意思是：仇人在狭窄的路上相遇，彼此无法回避。比喻不愿相见的人偏偏碰见，也比喻仇人相见，不肯放过。例如：劫匪与事主冤家路窄，狭路相逢，事主马上报警，"倒霉"劫匪落网！（《劫匪事主狭路相逢》，1990年10月27日《联合晚报》第24版）

这条俗语也可以倒过来说成"狭路相逢，冤家路窄"；也可以减省说成"狭路逢冤家"；还可以分开来单用，说成"狭路相逢"或"冤家路窄"。

Meeting The Enemies On A Narrow Path

"Yuanjia" refers to enemies or people whom you dislike or abhor. To meet them on a narrow path figuratively means there is no way of avoiding each other and there is bound to be a direct confrontation.

Example: "The robbery victim was literally 'meeting his enemies on a narrow road.' He spotted his assailants by accident and promptly alerted the police. The ill-fated robbers were nabbed instantly!" (Lianhe Wanbao 27/10/90)

远亲不如近邻 yuǎnqīn bùrú jìnlín

远亲：血统关系疏远的亲戚，这里指居住相隔很远的亲戚。近邻：邻居。全句的意思是远处的亲戚比不上住在近旁的邻居，指邻里关系更加密切，有困难，可以随时相互帮助。例如：近年来，澳洲人觉悟到自己的文化传统虽然源自英国，但是离得远。所谓远亲不如近邻，因此有需要跟亚洲各国发展关系。为此，政府计划在10年内在中小学普及亚洲语文的学习。（《澳洲政府鼓励学习华文》，1991年4月26日《联合早报》第17版）

这条俗语也说成"远亲不似近邻"或"远亲戚不如近边邻里"。也可以接着往下说，成为"远亲不如近邻，近邻不如对门"，并凝缩成"远亲近邻，不如对门"。

A Close Neighbour Is Better Than A Distant Relative

"Yuanqin" here refers to a relative who lives faraway. This Chinese proverb stresses the fact that in times of emergency, a neighbour nearby is more helpful than a relative staying a long way away.

Example: "In recent years, Australia is realising that despite its cultural affinity with England which is faraway, it needs to develop better relations with Asian countries, after all, 'a close neighbour is better than a distant relative'. Therefore, the government is now planning to popularise learning of Asian languages in schools within the next 10 years." (Lianhe Zaobao 26/4/91)

只听楼梯响，不见人下来

zhǐ tīng lóutī xiǎng, bù jiàn rén xiàlái

比喻嘴上说要有所行动，但是迟迟不见行动。例如：很长一段时间，苏联上层就传出将学习波兰的做法，举行圆桌会议，由各方面不同政见的人共同治国的说法。可是“只听楼梯响，不见人下来”，戈尔巴乔夫一直按兵不动。（《苏联的局势能缓和吗？》，1991年5月10日《联合早报》第19版）

这条俗语也说成“只听楼梯响，不见人下楼”、“只闻楼梯响，不见人下来”或“只听雷声响，不见雨下来”。

Words Have Not Been Followed By Deeds

Literally, this Chinese proverb means only heard the sound of steps, but fails to see someone coming down. It satirizes a person who does not back up his word with action.

Example: “The Soviet leadership has for sometime indicated its intention to follow the Polish system of round-table conference to allow people of different political affiliations to jointly run the country. However, ‘words have not been followed by deeds’, so far Gorbachev has not made any move toward that direction.” (Lianhe Zaobao 10/5/91)

事后诸葛亮 shìhòu Zhūgé Liàng

诸葛亮：三国时蜀汉政治家，帮助刘备建立蜀汉政权，小说《三国演义》对他的智谋大事渲染；后多用来泛指足智多谋的人。

这条俗语比喻事情发生（或处理、了结）之后才出主意、提建议或说现成话。例如：有82.2%的合格选民，参加了这次关系苏联前途的全民投票，投赞成票者占77%。戈尔巴乔夫似乎赢得相当轻松。然而，事后诸葛亮容易做，或许戈尔巴乔夫的确认为自己稳操胜券才倡议以全民投票方式决定苏联的前途。（《苏联全民投票结果剖析》，1991年3月21日《联合早报》第14版）

Be Wise After The Event

Zhuge Liang was a celebrated politician in Chinese history known for his wisdom and resourcefulness. This Chinese proverb satirizes someone who becomes a wise man only after an event has come to past.

Example: "In the referendum in Soviet Union recently, of the 88.2% eligible voters 77% supported President Gorbachev who seemed very sure of an easy victory. Perhaps he was merely trying to 'be wise after the event'. After all, he might have already known what the outcome would be." (Lianhe Zaobao 21/3/91)

做一日和尚敲一日钟　zuò yī rì héshang qiāo yī rì zhōng

“敲”也说“撞”，撞钟是和尚应做的事。比喻工作不起劲，消极应付，干一天算一天。

例如：一个人由于职业上的见惯听惯做惯，会产生好坏两种截然不同的效果。坏的方面是工作流于形式，做一日和尚敲一日钟。（《由“敲一日钟”到“烹小鲜”》，1991年7月14日《联合早报》第2版，“烹”：pēng，煮。）

“一日”也说“一天”或“日”。

To Carry Out One's Duty Unenthusiastically

Literally, this Chinese proverb means "one more day as a monk, toll the bell for just another day". It uses the monotony of a monk's daily duty to describe the indifferent and uninterested attitude of a worker.

Example: "After a worker has been engaged in a routine job over a long period of time, there are likely to be two entirely different effects: good and bad. The bad one is he may treat his job as a mere formality and 'carries out his duty unenthusiastically'." (Lianhe Zaobao 14/7/91)

拔头筹　bá tóuchóu

拔：夺取；头筹：第一。“拔头筹”就是“夺取第一（名）”。例如：1月17日“沙漠风暴”开战当夜，美国电缆电视新闻广播网（CNN）拔得头筹的幕后功臣，是台湾台扬科技公司出品的手提卫星电话。它使CNN在巴格达的三名记者，能克服电力和通讯上的障碍，把开火的消息传达给全球电视观众。（《台手提卫星电话·战地记者大派用场》，1991年2月7日《联合早报》第32版）

To Achieve The Leading Position

"Ba" means to attain; "touchou" is the first position. This Chinese idiom is used to describe someone who has excelled over others in a competition.

Example: "CNN 'achieved the leading position' in reporting the Desert Storm when the war broke out on January 17. Behind its success was the portable satellite phone produced by Taiwan's Tai Yang Sci-Tech Company. It enabled three CNN journalists to overcome electricity and communication interruptions and continued to transmit news of the war to its global audience. (Lianhe Zaobao 7/2/91)

半吊子 bàndiàozi

原本是上海话词语，已为华语词汇所吸收。

中国古代的铜钱一千枚穿成一串，叫一吊，半吊是五百，不能满吊。因此，“半吊子”比喻知识不丰富或技术不熟练的人。例如：蒋方良（蒋孝武的母亲）的生活圈子里有许多浙江奉化人，因此，她学到的是半吊子华语——带有俄国腔的宁波官话。（《没有声音的第一夫人》，1991年7月2日《联合晚报》第15版。这个例句中的“半吊子华语”指的是“不纯正的华语”。

“半吊子”还可以用来指以下三种人：（1）不通事理，说话随便的人；（2）做事有始无终的人；（3）说话不直爽的人。

Half A String Of Coins

In ancient China, coins were tied into a string for easy handling. This Shanghainese dialect describes someone who is only half a string, meaning he is not sufficiently knowledgeable or fully skilled.

Example: "Jiang Xiaowu's mother was a Russian. Although she learnt Chinese from the people in the area where she used to live, her Mandarin is like 'half a string of coins', with a strong Russian accent." (Lianhe Wanbao 2/7/91)

闭门羹 bìméngēng

宋代王铚（Wáng Zhì）写的《云仙杂记》第1卷《迷香洞》记载了这么一件事：

安徽（Ānhuī）宣城有个出了名的妓女叫史凤，她接客分等级。上等客人，就跟他们见面；下等客人，连见都不见，只用羹汤招待他们。羹是汤类食物，糊（hù）状，如豆腐羹、鱼翅羹。

拒绝客人进门，不跟来客相见，叫做请人家吃闭门羹；被关在门外，进不得门，叫做"吃闭门羹"。这条惯用语也可以用来比喻拒绝别人的要求或意见。例如：我国本年度七月歌台冠军司仪连环炮，几年前曾到台湾去闯天下。谁知到处碰壁吃闭门羹，三个月后就怀着一颗失落的心，垂头丧气地打算回家。（《闯宝岛吃闭门羹》，1990年11月19日《联合晚报》第2版）

Having The Door Slammed In One's Face

Literally, this Chinese proverb means "closed-door soup". It originated from an ancient story about a prostitute by the name of Shi Feng who divided her clients into different categories; good clients were well received while low-ranking clients were only given a bowl of soup outside her closed door.

To get a "closed-door soup" nowadays means to be declared persona non grata.

Example: "Singapore's award-winning compere Lian Huanpao went to Taiwan several years ago to develop his career, but he 'ate closed-door soup' wherever he went and dejectedly decided to return home three months later." (Lianhe Wanbao 19/11/90)

别苗头　bié miáotou

上海话词语。上海话里的"别"有好几个意思，其一可当"比"讲："苗头"一般有三个意思，一个是当"本领"或"办法"讲。因此，"别苗头"的意思是"比高低"，跟"竞争"同义。例如：两家潮剧团昨晚在同一时间、同一地点演戏酬神，又演同样的剧目《春草闯堂》，以较量演技，互别苗头，真是难得一见的有趣场面！（《同时同地剧目，两潮剧团演对台戏大斗演技》，1990年12月21日《联合晚报》第9版）

To Compare Each Other's Skills

It is a Shanghainese dialect. "Bie" means compare; "Miaotou" means capabilities or skills.

Example: "Two Teochew street operas staged the same show at the same time and place last night. It was interesting to watch how they competed with each other and 'compared each other's skills'." (Lianhe Wanbao 21/12/90)

擦屁股 cā pìgu

比喻替别人做收尾的工作（多指留下的难题或不好收拾的事），也说成“揩屁股”。例如：从1966年文革爆发到1976年毛泽东逝世，开过两次党代会，有数的几次中全会。毛泽东就在这几次会议上干掉了刘少奇和林彪两个“庞然（pángrán）大物”，干净利落，一点儿不用擦屁股。（《七中全会邓小平得到什么？》，1991年1月8日《联合早报》）

To Clean The Buttock

This Chinese proverb means to clean up after a dirty job has been undertaken by the person himself or by other people.

Example: “There were two party delegate meetings and numerous central committee meetings held during the beginning of the Cultural Revolution in 1966 and the death of Mao Zedong in 1976. Mao used the meetings to get rid of two political giants, Liu Shaoqi and Lin Biao. It was done with such expediency that he didn’t even have ‘to clean the buttock’.” (Lianhe Zaobao 8/1/91)

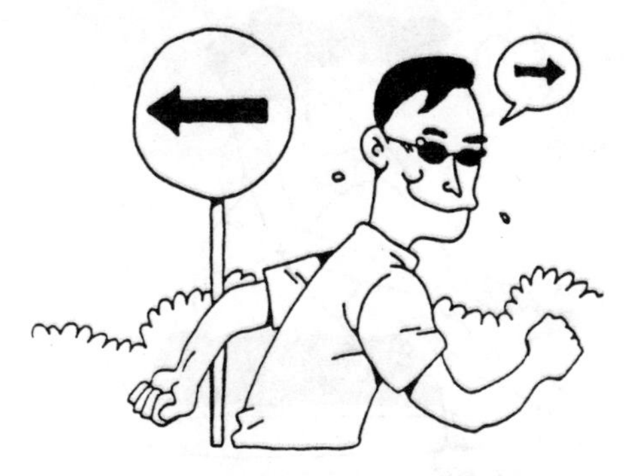

唱反调 chàng fǎndiào

原指唱相反的调子。比喻提出相反的主张，采取相反的行动。例如：看到自己的姓名以本民族的文字印在身分证上，谁都会有一份喜悦（yuè）和亲切感，虽然小部分唱反调的会说："姓名印在照片之下，简直就像通缉犯。"（《大受欢迎的措施》，1991年6月6日《新明日报》第8版）

To Sing A Different Tune

This Chinese term describes people who deliberately speak or act contrary to the wishes of the majority.

Example: "Although some people 'sang a different tune' by saying that to print one's name right under the photo made him look like a wanted person, for me it is delightful and gratifying to see my own Chinese name on the Identity Card." (Shin Min Daily News 6/6/91)

穿小鞋 chuān xiǎo xié

鞋子小，脚大，不跟脚，穿起来就受挤压，不舒服。“穿小鞋”是比喻暗地里耍手段，故意为难人或进行报复。例如：大凡敢乱摊派、乱收费、乱罚款的，都是掌握了一定权力的单位和领导干部。有的领导人，对敢抗“乱”的人，当面不敢怎样，背后便会给你穿小鞋。（《中国的“三乱”》，1991年6月14日《联合早报》第19版）

“小鞋”还有一种叫“玻璃小鞋”。“穿玻璃小鞋”是指受害者本人更不容易觉察的刁难（diāonàn，故意使人为难）或报复。

To Make A Person Wear Tight Shoes

This Chinese term means to insidiously put someone in a tight spot or to cause him troubles.

Example: “In China, those who apportion expenses, impose charges and fines without proper reasons are usually government corporations and party cadres possessing some authority. Those who dare to go against them were secretly ‘made to wear tight shoes’.” (Lianhe Zaobao 14/6/91)

打哈哈 dǎhāha

北京话词语，有两个意思，一是指开玩笑，一是指敷衍(fūyǎn，表面上应付一下)。例如：中英就香港兴建新机场问题，昨日举行新一轮会谈。记者除获准在会前拍照外，并没有其他采访安排，会议情况双方严格保密。中方组长罗嘉骥（huān）说，他从来都是个乐观主义者，对记者的其他问题则一律打哈哈。（《中国要多了解港新机场工程情况》，1991年2月22日《联合早报》第31版）。这个例句中的"打哈哈"，是"敷衍"、"应付"的意思。

To Make Casual Remarks

This Chinese term is a Beijing dialect which has two meanings: (a) to crack a joke; (b) to make casual remarks perfunctorily.

Example: "China and Britain held another round of meetings over Hongkong's proposed airport project yesterday. The press was barred except for taking pictures. Both countries' representatives were required to keep the proceedings strictly confidential and China's head of delegate, Mr Luo Jiahuan, merely 'made casual remarks' whenever he was asked for comments." (Lianhe Zaobao 22/2/91)

大锅饭　dàguōfàn

中国在1958年大跃进时期大搞“人民公社化”运动，农村办起大量的食堂，农民自己家里不煮饭，都到食堂去吃饭，叫“吃大锅饭”，所以“大锅饭”是指大锅里做的为多数人提供的普通伙食。后用“大锅饭”或“吃大锅饭”来比喻分配上的平均主义，即不管多干少干、干好干坏、干与不干，报酬都一样。例如：在社会主义制度下生活久了的前东德人，习惯了那种吃不饱、饿不死的“稳定”。“大锅饭”这剂万灵丹，40年来使他们都吃得上那么一口粥。可是，现在的情况完全不同了。（《遥遥无期的美丽新世界——东西德统一后面对诸多问题》，1991年4月24日《联合早报》第17版）

A Huge Cauldron Of Food

In 1958, when China launched the “Great Leap Forward” campaign, communes were set up where everyone had to have their daily meals from the same canteen. This was later known as “a huge cauldron of food”. It was aimed at putting the idea of “equal work and equal benefit” into practice.

Example: “The East Germans who used to struggle under the socialist system, have found out after 40 years that ‘a huge cauldron of food’ was not a panacea to their problems. However, things are entirely different now.” (Lianhe Zaobao 24/4/91)

二进宫　èrjìngōng

原本是京剧剧目，比喻第二次被拘留或进监狱。例如：一位工作人员说，这些瘾君子经过一段时间的治疗，（毒瘾）大部分被戒断，但也有一些毒瘾复发，不得不“二进宫”。（《云南瑞丽戒毒所见闻》，1991年4月25日《联合早报》第28版）

To Be Detained For The Second Time

It was originally the title of a Chinese opera, which means to be arrested or imprisoned for the second time.

Example: “An official said most of the drug addicts gave up their habits after a certain period of rehabilitation, but there were some who had ‘to be detained for the second time’.” (Lianhe Zaobao 25/4/91)

放空气　fàng kōngqì

比喻故意散布某种言论或消息。例如：伊拉克把中国外长钱其琛这次访问巴格达称为重要的访问。从伊拉克近日放出的空气看来，它会要求中国保证不向伊拉克开战，否决美国会在安理会提出的授权动武决议。（香港《明报》社评：《中国地位受尊重》，1990年11月14日《新明日报》第7版）

"放空气"也比喻故意制造某种气氛。

To Drop A Hint Publicly

Literally, this Chinese saying means to "let out air". It refers figuratively to an act of creating a general impression or dropping a hint.

Example: "Iraq describes the arrival of Chinese foreign minister Qian Qichen in Baghdad as an important visit. It is actually 'dropping a hint publicly' that it wants China to guarantee not to declare war against Iraq and to veto the United States' proposal at the UN Security Council to use force against the country." (Shin Min Daily News 14/11/90)

掼纱帽 guàn shāmào

上海话词语。掼：扔、摔；纱帽：也叫"乌纱"或"乌纱帽"，是中国古代文官戴的一种帽子，因此常用来作为官职的代称。

掼纱帽比喻因对工作不满而甩手（shuǎishǒu）不干，也比喻因气愤而辞职。例如：一人掼纱帽，惊动全世界。这可是世界上的大事情。美国部长、英国大臣等等下台，掼纱帽，被撵 (niǎn，驱逐，赶走）是常有的事，也从来没有象谢瓦尔德纳泽外长这次辞职那么紧张。（《谢瓦尔德纳泽为什么掼纱帽？》，1990年12月24日《联合早报》第9版）

To Throw Away One's Official Hat

"Guan" means to throw away; "Shamao" is a hat worn by feudal officials in ancient China. This proverb figuratively means to give up one's official post in great anger.

Example: "It was very rare that when one person 'threw away his official hat' and the whole world was shocked. Many American or British ministers have left their posts in a similar manner in the past, but none have caused so much concern as in the case of Soviet Foreign Minister Shevardnadze." (Lianhe Zaobao 24/12/90)

滚雪球 gǔn xuěqiú

本是下雪天的一种游戏，在雪地上滚动成团的雪，使体积愈来愈大。比喻人员或财富逐渐增加，也可以比喻联络的范围越来越大。例如：中国在内部稳住阵脚后，也想突破西方的抵制。钱其琛应邀访美，英、日外长同步访问北京，法国外长杜玛不久也将访问北京。这种滚雪球的形势，将使中国快速突破外交的孤立。（《东北亚强权关系的新发展》，1991年4月11日《联合早报》第15版）。这个例子中的"滚雪球"指跟中国恢复友好往来的国家越来越多。

Snowballing

This Chinese term is similar in meaning to the English word, which is to gather momentum or accumulate wealth gradually.

Example: "As the domestic situation stabilises, China is striving to overcome economic sanction by the West. Foreign minister Qian Qichen has accepted an invitation to visit us; while British, French and Japanese foreign ministers are arriving in Beijing. The snowballing of diplomatic goodwill might help China to break out of its present isolation." (Lianhe Zaobao 12/4/91)

后遗症 hòuyízhèng

原本指疾病痊愈后留下来的一些症状，比喻因为做事情或处理问题不认真、不妥当而留下的消极影响。例如：波斯湾战争暂时停息，国际上各种势力又重新开始了建立新秩序的努力。尤其是苏美二强，都在尽量消除战争期间因产生歧见而留下的后遗症。（《战火停息后的思考》，1991年3月4日《联合早报》第8版）

Unfavourable Consequences

Medically, this Chinese term refers generally to any ill-effects resulting from a severe sickness.

It is now also commonly used to describe any difficulties or sticky problems brought about by a major occurrence.

Example: "After the Gulf War ceasefire, major international powers are renewing their efforts to establish a new order. The US and the Soviet Union, the two superpowers especially are striving to resolve their differences and the 'unfavourable consequences' of the war." (Lianhe Zaobao 4/3/91)

节骨眼　jiēguyǎn

北京话词语，比喻关键时刻。例如：江泽民访问苏联，15日的德国电台几乎每一个小时都重复着这一消息，报纸也以重要版位刊载。这说明世界上两个最大国家的首脑相聚是多么重要，尤其在目前这个节骨眼上。（《评江泽民苏联之行》，1991年5月18日《联合早报》第17版）

"节骨眼"也比喻能起决定作用的环节。

这条惯用语也说成"接骨眼"或"骨节眼"，"眼"通常说成"眼儿"。

The Critical Moment

This Chinese term is a Beijing dialect which literally means the eye of a joint. It refers figuratively to a critical juncture.

Example: "When Jiang Zemin visited the Soviet Union, the German radio repeatedly reported the news almost every hour, and the newspapers also devoted much space to report it. This shows that when leaders of the two largest nations meet, especially at 'this critical moment', it is something really significant." (Lianhe Zaobao 18/5/91)

捞一票 lāoyīpiào

指用不正当的手段取得一笔可观的钱财或一批物资，也指在政治上或军事上取得某种利益。例如：耶尔辛趁戈尔巴乔夫去东京访问时也来到西欧，本想得到各国支持，在议会上好好捞上一票，谁知道碰了一鼻子灰。（《苏联的局势能缓和吗？》，1991年5月10日《联合早报》第19版）

这个句子里的“捞一票”用的是上述第二个意思。

这条惯用语也说成“捞一把”。

To Reap Some Benefits

It refers to an improper action to obtain a sum of money or to gain some profits. Politically or militarily, it can also mean to acquire a certain kind of intangible benefits.

Example: “Yeltsin went to Western Europe while Gorbachev was in Tokyo. He was hoping to win foreign support so as to ‘reap some benefits’ in the parliament, but he was rudely snubbed instead.” (Lianhe Zaobao 10/5/91)

婆婆妈妈 pópomāmā

形容人说话啰啰唆唆，做事慢手慢脚。例如：黄奕（yì）良说："如果你认识我，你会知道我一向不是个婆婆妈妈的人。现在，唉，我只能用一个'乱'字形容。"（《黄奕良日子过得乱七八糟》，1991年7月4日《联合早报》《影艺》版）

"婆婆妈妈"也可以形容容易动感情。

"婆婆妈妈事"是指家庭中男人认为不值得做的琐碎杂务。

Womanishly Fussy

Literally, this Chinese idiom means "behaving like mother and grandmother". It is used to describe people who are long-winded and clumsy, or are overly sentimental.

Example: "Huang Yiliang said those who know him should understand that he is not a person who is 'womanishly fussy'. But, right now I am really confused." (Lianhe Zaobao 4/7/91)

破天荒　pòtiānhuāng

中国唐朝时候，荆州每年送举人去考进士，都没考中，当时叫做天荒（从未开垦过的土地）。后来有个叫刘锐的考中了，就叫做破天荒。因此，破天荒是比喻事情第一次出现。例如：星期一，在英国海运历史上，一群姑娘破天荒成为第一批皇家海军战舰上的全职女水兵。（《一群英国女子参加海军》，1990年10月10日《联合早报》第29版）

Breaking The Virgin Land

In the Tang dynasty of China, the city of Jing sent candidates to sit for the highest imperial examinations annually, but not a single success had been reported. The place was described as "tian huang", or virgin land. Later, a candidate, Liu Rui broke the record by being the first person to pass, so the virgin land was thus "broken". The episode is now used to refer to anything that happens for the very first time.

Example: "On Monday, a group of females broke the virgin land by becoming the first batch of full-time servicewomen on board the Royal Navy's warship, thus setting a precedence in British naval history." (Lianhe Zaobao 10/10/90)

全武行 quánwǔháng

武行：戏曲中专门表演武打的角色。全武行是指戏曲中规模较大的武打，比喻打群架（双方聚集许多人打架）。

1月3日，台湾立法院开会。民进党立法委员张修逸（yì）为了报国民党资深立委张鸿学一拳之仇，企图上前打他，但是遭到好几位国民党立委的阻止，于是双方扭打成一团。1月4日《联合早报》在报道这条新闻时，标题是"台湾立法院又演全武行"（见第10版）。

"演全武行"跟"演铁公鸡"同义，都指打架，但是，前者常用来形容打群架，后者泛指打架，不论人数多少。

A Grand Show Of Fightings

"Wuhang" refers to actors in Chinese operas whose role is to engage in fighting. This Chinese proverb describes a show where all the actors are fighters; meaning: a large-scale fighting.

On the 3rd of January, Taiwan's opposition legislator Zhang Xiuyi attempted to punch Zhang Hongxue of the ruling party in retaliation, but was restrained by other Guomindang members. Both sides ended up in a big brawl. Lianhe Wanbao on 4/1/91 headlined, "Taiwan's Legislative Assembly puts up 'a grand show of fightings' again" to describe the incident.

杀手锏 shāshǒujiǎn

锏：中国古代的一种兵器，用金属做成，属鞭类。旧小说在描述格斗时，突然用锏投掷（zhì，音致）敌手的招数叫“杀手锏”。“杀”原本用“撒”字，“撒”读sā：“撒手”：放开手、松手。

“杀手锏”比喻在关键时刻使出最拿手的招数（也说成“着数”〔zhaōshù〕）。例如：台湾的老板在劳资对抗中，往往用金钱和权力玩弄法令，压制劳方，而且最后总以“关厂”为杀手锏来威胁（wēixié）工人，因此，有“资方有退路劳方无退路”的说法。（《台湾民间如何看待中国统一问题》，1990年11月30日《联合早报》第25版）

An Unexpected Thrust With The Mace

"Jian" is a type of ancient Chinese weapon with a sharp, whip-like point. In ancient novels, it was always used as the final and most lethal weapon to lance at the enemy at the critical moment.

Example: "In the labour-management confrontation in Taiwan, the employers frequently use money and power to go round labour regulations and suppress the workers: they also resort to 'factory closure' as 'an unexpected thrust with the mace' to threaten them. It is therefore often said that 'the management has a trump card and the labour has none'." (Lianhe Zaobao 30/11/90)

死胡同　sǐhútòng

胡同：小小街道，在中国南方多叫做“巷”，北京和北方一些城市叫“胡同”。死：不能通过。“死胡同”的原义是走不通的小巷子，比喻绝路；也叫“死巷子”。例如：苏联今天正处在三岔（chà）路口。一条是走回头路，一条是逐步完善社会主义，第三条是往右，走进历史的死胡同，倒退100年，变成最发达国家的原料附庸（fùyōng）。（《苏联改革面对的问题》，1991年3月20日《联合早报》第15版）

The Blind Alley

"Hutong" is a narrow lane usually with a dead end. This Chinese term describes a little lane that leads to nowhere.

Example: "The Soviet Union is now facing three possible options: one is back track, the second is to gradually perfect the existing socialist system, and the last is to turn right: going back 100 years to the historical 'blind alley', and becoming a vassal to the developed countries as their material supplier." (Lianhe Zaobao 20/3/91)

叹苦经 tànkǔjīng

上海话词语，意思是向人家诉说困难的情形，也说成“叹苦境”。

波斯湾战争爆发使法国巴黎专门经营高级时装的公司生意大减。一方面它们的订单被取消，另一方面，一批老主顾——阿拉伯公主及石油大亨（dàhēng）的太太不再向他们订购高级时装。巴黎时装公司商会主席莫克里尔说：目前的情况糟透了。1991年1月24日《联合早报》在报道这条新闻时，标题是《油国王子公主不见了！巴黎时装界叹苦经》（第7版）。

To Tell A Woeful Story

This Chinese idiom is actually a Shanghainese dialect which means to pour out one's sorrows.

The Gulf War has severely affected high fashion houses in Paris as many orders have been cancelled and their major clients, the Arab princesses and oil tycoons have stopped patronising them. The Paris Fashion House Association complained that things simply could not be worse.

Describing their predicament, Lianhe Wanbao on 24/1/91 headlined: "Princes and princesses from oil kingdoms have disappeared, Paris fashion houses 'telling woeful stories'."

趟浑水 tāng húnshuǐ

趟：从浅水里走过去；浑水：混浊的水。比喻跟着别人干坏事。例如：中国现在正极力谋求与西方国家改善关系，应该知道只要帮助任何一个回教国家发展核武器，都会再次得罪整个西方世界，并将使大家的关系在今后十年内难以打破僵局，所以中国绝不会轻易**趟**这种**浑水**。(《世界军火交易中的中国话题》，1991年5月8日《联合早报》第16版)

To Wade In Muddy Waters

This Chinese idiom means to follow others in committing evil doings.

Example: "China is striving to improve its relations with the West and should know that to assist any muslim country develop nuclear weapons is sure to antagonize the western world and thereby stiffen the relationship for perhaps another 10 years. China is most unlikely to want 'to wade in such muddy waters'." (Lianhe Zaobao 8/5/91)

套近乎 tào jìnhu

北京话词语，也说“拉近乎”或“找近乎”，意思是跟不太熟或不很密切的人拉拢关系，主动表示亲近。常含贬(biǎn)义。例如：中国在今日国际政治舞台的影响力绝非任何发展中国家可以同日而语，甚至一般的发达国家也难以相提并论。中国强调自己与马来西亚、菲律宾、寮国（Liáoguó）及斯里兰卡同属发展中国家，更多的是为了套近乎。不这样，中国又怎能和东南亚地区国家结为一体呢？（《中国外交战略的新态势》，1990年12月12日《联合早报》第12版）

To Get Closer To

This Chinese term originating from the Beijing dialect describes a deliberate act to promote closer relations or to establish proximity with someone. It is often used in a derogatory sense.

Example: “China's influence in the international political arena today is far greater than any other developing countries, perhaps even greater than many developed countries. The fact that it is openly identifying itself with Malaysia, the Philippines, Laos and Sri Lanka is actually 'to get closer to' them. Isn't it the best way for China to promote unity with these countries?” (Lianhe Zaobao 12/12/90)

挑大梁 tiǎodàliáng

挑：支撑。大梁：也叫正梁，即脊檩（jílǐn），架在屋架或山墙上面最高的一根横木。

挑大梁有两个意思：（1）指在戏剧等艺术表演中担任主角或主要演员。（2）指承担重任或负责主要工作。

例如：环境剧《我们的生活在这里》。钱治刚挑大梁（标题，1991年3月20日《新明日报》第13版）。这个例子中的“挑大梁”用的是上述第一个意思，新闻说，在新广7月1日启播的新环境剧《我们的生活在这里》中，钱治刚将扮演剧中的主要人物。

“挑大梁”也说成“挑正梁”。

To Shoulder The Main Beam

This Chinese term has two meanings: (1) To play the main role in a stage performance; (2) to undertake the main task.

Example: “In ‘We are living here’, a show to promote green environment, actor Qian Zhigang ‘shoulders the main beam’.” (Shin Min Daily News 20/3/91)

铁公鸡 tiěgōngjī

铁公鸡：用铁铸（zhù）成的公鸡，拔不下一根毛来；本是歇后语"铁公鸡——一毛不拔"的省略形式。比喻非常吝啬(lìnsè)。

铁公鸡也是京剧的一个剧目，全武行（quánwǔháng）——规模较大的武打，因此，又比喻大打出手，常跟"演"字连用。本地报章常用"铁公鸡"的这个比喻义。例如：一名印族青年因车祸受重伤，送进医院后不久就去世。他的家人和已经分居的妻子却各自带领一批人争领遗体，双方在医院险些演出一场铁公鸡。（《争领尸体·险演铁公鸡》，1990年11月23日《新明日报》第13版）。

Iron Rooster

This Chinese term was used originally in a two-part allegorical saying which meant extremely stingy: as an iron rooster has not even a single feather to spare.

It later became the title of an opera which involved large-scale hand-to-hand fighting, and is now used commonly to describe clashes between two parties.

Example: "An Indian youth died from a road accident in the hospital and his family and separated wife led two groups of people to claim his body. In the ensuing quarrel they almost end up with an 'iron rooster' show." (Shin Min Daily News 23/11/90)

挖墙脚　wā qiángjiǎo

墙脚：墙的根基。挖墙脚是比喻暗地里耍（shuǎ）手段破坏别人的事。例如：如果作栋失败，对显龙会产生不利的影响，因为他跟作栋的关系太过密切。如果他挖作栋的墙脚，等于挖自己的墙脚。（李光耀总理在行动党干部大会上的演讲，1990年11月26日《联合早报》第6版）

"挖墙脚"也说成"挖墙角"或"掏墙角"，"掏"（tāo，音涛）跟"挖"同义。

"挖墙角"跟口语中的"拆台"（chāitái）同义，因此，还可以说成"拆墙角"。

华语中有个词儿叫"挖角"（wājué），意思是把别的戏班里优秀的演员用较高的薪酬或别的手段拉到自己的戏班里来，也比喻拉走别的团体或机构的人员。"挖墙角"的另一个意思跟"挖角"相同。

To Dig At The Foot Of Someone's Wall

Literally, this Chinese idiom means to undermine the foundation of a building. Generally, it is used to describe an action to cut the ground under someone's feet.

Example: "Mr Lee Kuan Yew said that if Chok Tong failed, it would have adverse effect on Hsien Loong, because their relationship was too close. If Hsien Loong 'dug at the foot of Chok Tong's wall', he would actually be digging at his own wall." (Lianhe Zaobao 26/9/90)

无底洞 wúdǐdòng

永远填不满的洞，比喻要求或欲望很多，怎么也不能满足。例如：西方国家虽然有意帮助戈尔巴乔夫，但最终是否能给苏联一大笔援助，还取决于苏联本身政经局势的发展，因为没有人愿意把钱朝无底洞里扔。（《乌龙翻译误导出的千亿美元援苏案》，1991年5月28日《联合早报》第14版）

A Bottomless Pit

It figuratively describes an insatiable demand or unrealisable expectation.

Example: "The western countries are prepared to help Mr Gorbachev financially, but ultimately it would depend on the political and economic developments in the Soviet Union because nobody is willing to throw money into 'a bottomless pit'." (Lianhe Zaobao 28/5/91)

西洋镜 xīyángjìng

原本是中国民间的一种文娱活动方式，北方农村叫拉洋片或拉大片。把各种各样的画片放在一个木箱里上下拉动或左右移动，表演者说唱画面的内容，观众从透镜里看到放大的画面。因为画片都是西洋画，所以也叫做“西洋景”。

“西洋镜”是比喻故意要弄使人难以捉摸的花招来骗人的事物或手法，常跟“拆穿”或“戳（chuō）穿”连用。例如：四个大男人怂恿丽莎“参股”，说是出4万元可赚一倍。丽莎很精，一面敷衍应酬，一面推托说没这么多钱。这伙人一再减价，还邀丽莎去神庙发誓，并结为兄妹，同进共退。丽莎终于忍不住当面拆穿他们的西洋镜，大骂一顿。（《阿梅遭遇变态狂·丽莎计退大老千》，1990年10月22日《联合早报》第5版）

Western Glasses

Originally it referred to a form of popular entertainment in villages in China years ago in which pictures of western scenery were manipulated in a wooden box to give them an animated effect. Viewers had to look into the box through holes covered with glasses. The visual manipulation was later likened to a trick or deception. To uncover the “western glasses” nowadays means to expose a trick or a deception.

Example: “Liza was approached by four conmen for a joint business venture and was told that she could double her income with $40,000 investment. Cleverly, she used various excuses to extricate herself and finally exposed their ‘western glasses’.” (Lianhe Wanbao 22/10/90)

夜猫子 yèmaozi

夜猫子就是猫头鹰，它的活动规律是白天躲起来，晚上出来活动；常用来比喻喜欢晚睡的人。例如：10点起是迪斯科时间，再加上一段时装表演，客人在午夜零时散去。有夜猫子，当然也有早起的鸟儿。清晨赶往北京的公园，可以看到许多人在打太极拳，做操或跳老人迪斯科。（《北京人的最新乐子》，1990年11月20日《联合早报》第18版。乐子：lèzi，北京方言词语，令人快乐的事儿。）

Cat Of The Night

It actually refers to the owl and is used in this Chinese metaphor to liken people who are extraordinarily active at night, especially in social activities.

Example: "The disco starts at 10 pm, with a fashion show, the guests would normally stay till the wee hours. These 'cats of the night' are in contrast to the early birds who turn up at gardens in Beijing at dawn to do taiji or other morning exercises." (Lianhe Wanbao 20/11/90)

有两下子 yǒu liǎng xiàzi

我国著名的女保龄球运动员吕宝玲，虽然身材娇小，但是球艺纯熟，比赛时斗志昂扬，有一股辣劲。《联合早报星期刊》体育版在介绍吕宝玲时，文章的标题是："小辣椒"有两下子。（1991年5月19日第20版）"有两下子"常用在口语里，意思是"有些本领"；也说成"有两手"。

Have Unusual Skills

This is a common spoken term which describes someone having impressive skills.

It was used in the headline in Lianhe Zaobao (19/5/91) to describe the outstanding performance of Singapore's bowling star, Lu Baoling, who is petite but vigorous and skilful.

The headline was: "Little Chilli Padi, really has unusual skills".

冤大头 yuāndàtóu

北京话词语。冤：吃亏、上当；大头：指容易吃亏上当的人。

"冤大头"指白费钱财的人。例如：过去，华人一向只问捐款，从来不好意思要求回馈（huí kuì，也叫反馈）。最近几年，华人开始体会出老当冤大头失策，逐渐也会用钞票去和政客们周旋（zhōuxuán，交际应酬）。（《美国华人社会何去何从》，1991年6月25日《联合早报》第15版）

"冤大头"也指无缘无故受人欺骗或侮辱（wǔrǔ）的人。

这条惯用语也说成"冤大脑袋"或"大头"。

People Who Lavished Money For Nothing

This Chinese term refers to people who have been cheated and suffered losses as a result.

Example: "In the past, American Chinese used to make political donations but never asked for anything in return. In recent years, however, they realised that they should not continue to be 'people who lavished money for nothing'. They are now using money to influence politicians." (Lianhe Zaobao 25/6/91)

执牛耳 zhí niú ěr

中国古代诸侯订立盟约时，主持盟会的人要亲手割下牛的耳朵取血，然后把它放在盘子里，让参加盟会的人都尝一点，表示有诚意、守信用。“执牛耳”本来是指盟主，后用来泛指在某一领域占居领导地位。例如：经过这场中东战争，美国和其他西方盟国一定扶持埃及，穆巴拉可能拾起纳塞的棒子，成为执中东地区牛耳的强人。（《谁是波斯湾战争的大赢家和输家？》，1991年3月9日《联合早报》第11版）

“执牛耳”也说成“操牛耳”，“操”（cāo）当“抓”、“拿”讲。

Holding A Leading Position

This Chinese term originated from an ancient ceremony at which a prince would hold a plate containing the blood from the ears of a sacrificial bull for tasting by everyone present to mark the conclusion of an alliance. It is now used to signify a person holding a leading position.

Example: “After the Gulf War, US and its western allies are sure to give Egypt their strong support. President Mubarak may therefore succeed Naser to become a strongman ‘holding a leading position’ in the Middle East.” (Lianhe Zaobao 9/3/91)

走过场 zǒu guòchǎng

过场：演戏的时候，角色一上场就穿过舞台从另一边下场。“走过场”是比喻办事只讲形式，不讲效果，随便应付一下就算了。例如：上至中央，下至地方，中国当局都曾说过严禁乱摊派、乱收费、乱罚款。最近广东省当局也发出通知，表示要整顿“三乱”。但是老百姓普遍认为，这不过是官样文章，到头来还不是走过场。（《中国的“三乱”》，1991年6月14日《联合早报》第19版）

To Go Through The Motions

This Chinese term describes a performance in an opera in which the actor merely passes through the stage.

It's now used to mean making a gesture to give the impression of doing something which in fact is only a formality.

Example: "The central as well as the provincial authorities have publicly announced the banning of unauthorised apportionment of expenses, imposition of charges and fines. However, in Guangdong province, the people generally believe that the announcements were merely 'to go through the motions,' nothing will happen in practice." (Lianhe Zaobao 14/6/91)

坐冷板凳 zuò lĕngbăndèng

比喻因不受重视而长期清闲。

1988年在汉城举行的奥运会上，中国乒乓球队的女运动员陈静荣获女子单打冠军，可是，这位奥运金牌得主已经一年没有参加国际赛了。最近，也未能获选参加在吉隆坡举行的第10届亚洲乒乓球锦标赛。《新明日报》在报道这一则新闻时，用了这样的标题："奥运乒赛女单冠军·陈静坐冷板凳"（1990年12月12日第22版）。这个标题中的"坐冷板凳"，用的就是上述比喻义。

如果因不受重视而担任清闲的职位，或者想进见某人而受冷落，又或者长期等候差遣 (chāiqiăn)，也都可以用"坐冷板凳"来形容。

Made To Sit On A Cold Wooden Stool

This is the literal translation of the Chinese saying which is used generally to describe a person who holds a substantial position or a recognised title but is not given any job to keep him suitably occupied.

For example, Chinese Olympic table tennis gold medalist, Chen Jing who has not taken part in any international competition for more than a year, again failed to appear at the 10th Asian Table Tennis Tournament in K.L.

In a news article headlined: "Chinese Olympic table tennis woman single champion Chen Jing 'made to sit on a cold wooden stool'," Shin Min Daily News (12/12/90) used the idiom to metaphorically describe her position.

做文章 zuò wénzhāng

比喻抓住一件事发议论或在上面打主意。例如：从1980年中共决定设立深圳、珠海、汕头、厦门4个经济特区，1988年又开放从北到南14个沿海大中港口城市，到1988年提出沿海经济发展战略，中国的开放格局基本上是在沿海地区做文章。（《中国对外开放新格局》，1990年12月18日《联合早报》第21版）。所谓“在沿海地区做文章”就是在沿海地区打主意。

“做”也写成“作”。

To Make An Issue Of Something/ To Undertake Major Activities

Literally, this Chinese idiom means to write an essay. Metaphorically, it describes an action to make an issue of something or to undertake major activities on certain project.

Example: "The Chinese government established 4 Special Economic Zones in 1980 in Shenzhen, Zhuhai, Shantou and Xiamen and opened up 14 coastal cities from north to south in 1988 as its main coastal economic development strategy. Basically, its Open Policy is 'to undertake major activities' along the coastal areas." (Lianhe Zaobao 18/12/90)

赶鸭子上架　gǎn yāzi shàng jià

架：架子，是用来放器物或支撑物体等等的工具，如报架、书架、床架、货架等。

这条歇后语的后段是“有意作难”（zuònán，为难），所以引用这条歇后语是比喻勉强别人去做能力够不上的事情。例如：六四事件之后，中共一个劲儿的开中央全会，究竟解决了多少问题？四中全会、五中全会尤有可说，江泽民“赶鸭子上架”，当了总书记，当了中央军委主席。但有名无实，谁来当都一样的。就接班而言，并不算解决了问题。（《七中全会邓小平得到什么？》，1991年1月8日《联合早报》第13版）

To Drive A Duck Onto A Perch

This is the first part of a Chinese two-part allegorical saying which means to make someone do a job that is entirely beyond his capability. The second part means “to purposely put him in a difficult position”.

Example: “After the Tiananmen Square incident, the Chinese Communist Party held numerous meetings. What have they managed to solve? Jiang Zemin was like ‘a duck driven onto a perch’. As the Secretary General and Chairman of the Central Military Commission, he is actually powerless. As far as the question of political succession is concerned, no solution is yet in sight.” (Lianhe Zaobao 8/1/91)

两股道上跑的车，走的不是一条路

liǎng gǔ dàoshang pǎo de chē, zǒu de bù shì yī tiáo lù

这条歇后语比喻各自的目标不同，所选择的道路也不一样。例如：现在，戈尔巴乔夫要在苏联实现“人道的民主的社会主义”，邓小平则要在中国建设“有中国特色的社会主义”，二者表面看来是两股道上跑的车，走的不是一条路。但在实质上，二者都难言是如假包换的社会主义，殊途同归的可能性并非不存在。（《中苏关系新模式》，1991年5月22日《联合早报》第17版）

“走的不是一条路”也说“走的不是一条道儿”。

Same Tracks But Different Routes

Literally, this Chinese saying means two cars racing on the same tracks may not actually be taking the same routes. It emphasizes the fact that people with different objectives may not adopt the same approaches to achieve them.

Example: “Gorbachev wants to practise “humanitarian democratic socialism”, whereas Deng Xiaoping is keen on establishing a “unique Chinese socialism.” They seem to be on the “same tracks but different routes”. However, they are basically socialism in substance and may eventually prove to be reaching for the same destination”. (Lianhe Zaobao 22/5/91)

聋子对话 lóngzi duìhuà

这条歇后语的后段（语底）是“自说自话”。“自说自话”是上海方言词语，有两个意思：（1）自作主张；（2）自言自语。跟“聋子对话”相组合，“自说自话”应理解为各说各的，无法沟通与回应。

1月9日，美国国务卿贝克和伊拉克外长阿齐士在日内瓦洲际酒店举行会谈。“在会谈之前，有人预料可能只谈5分钟而破裂散会，也有人说可能是一次“聋子对话”，双方自说自话，于对方之言听而不闻。（《从胡申的个性去推测》（时事漫谈），1991年1月12日《联合早报》第16版）

The Deaf Talking To Each Other

This Chinese idiom originated from a two-part allegorical saying which satirizes two persons talking at cross purposes and there was no way of communicating effectively with each other.

Example: "On the 9 of January, US Secretary of State, James Baker and Iraqi Foreign Minister, Tareq Aziz met in Geneva. Before the talk, there were predictions that either the talk would break down within five minutes, or it might merely be 'the deaf talking to each other'; as neither party was prepared to listen to what the other had to say." (Lianhe Zaobao 12/1/91)

秋后的蚱蜢，蹦个没几天了

qiū hòu de zhàměng, bèng gè méi jǐ tiān le

蚱蜢：也叫蚂蚱（màzha），像蝗虫，危害农作物，活不过冬天。蹦：跳。这条歇后语是比喻离死亡不远了。例如：在中国现代史上最具传奇色彩的英雄人物、西安事变的主角张学良将军，幽居55年后，最近终于飞到美国探亲，与家人团聚。他在离台前，很风趣地把自己比作秋后的蚱蜢，蹦个没几天了，所以乘跑得动的时候出国看看。（《张学良真正有了自由》，1991年3月13日《联合早报》第15版）

这条歇后语的后段（语底）也说成："还能蹦几蹦"，"没几天蹦跶(bèngda)了"，"蹦跶不了几天了"，"日子长不了"，"跳不长了"，"眼看就要完蛋了"或"等着伸腿（死亡）吧"。

Like A Grasshopper At The End Of Autumn, Its Days Are Numbered

As grasshoppers cannot survive the winter, by the end of autumn, they don't have much longer time to hop around and to cause trouble. This Chinese proverb means someone, especially the enemy is on his last legs.

Example: "The most legendary hero in China's modern history, General Zhang Xueliang flew to the US to visit his relatives after under house arrest for 55 years. Before his departure form Taipei, he humorously likened himself to 'a grasshopper at the end of autumn, its days are numbered', meaning he did not have much time to travel around." (Lianhe Zaobao 13/3/91)

丈八金刚摸不到头脑 zhàng bā Jīngāng mōbudào tóunǎo

这条歇后语的语面是“丈八金刚”，语底是“摸不到头脑”，意思是摸身高一丈八尺的金刚的头，当然摸不着咯。比喻一时不知事情的经过，弄不清底細（dǐxi）或原因。例如：元代的陶瓷器多流落到南洋一带，但是现有的元代史籍都不够完整，南洋的地名又译得不恰当，这一切把研究元代陶瓷的人弄得丈八金刚摸不到头脑。（《郑俊杰走遍20多国・发现800多件元代陶瓷》，1991年2月19日《联合早报》第6版）

这条歇后语理的“金刚”也说成“和尚”，“丈八”也说成“丈二”；“摸不到”一般都说成“摸不着”。

Unable To Get To The Bottom Of Things

“Zhang” is an unit of length which is about 3.5 metres. Literally, this Chinese proverb means the statue of a Buddhist monk which is 1.8 zhang is so tall that it is difficult to reach for its head. Figuratively, it means something occurs unexpectedly and its causes remain puzzling or cannot be explained.

Example: “Many pottery and porcelain wares of the Yuan dynasty were found in SE Asia, but there are few historical records on their origins and researchers are ‘unable to get to the bottom of things’.” (Lianhe Zaobao 19/2/91)